Hope for the Overcomers Soul

Presented by LaKesha L. Williams

HOPE FOR THE OVERCOMERS SOUL
Copyright © 2018 by LaKesha L. Williams

All scripture quotations are public domain courtesy of Bible Gateway: www.biblegateway.com

All Rights Reserved. No part of this publication may be reproduced, stored in a retrieval system, or transmitted in any form or by any means, electronic, mechanical, photocopying or otherwise, without the prior permission of the copyright owner.

ISBN: 978-1-7327674-0-9
Library of Congress Control #2018913080

Edited by Latricia C. Bailey of LCB Enterprises

Vision to Fruition Publishing House
www.vision-fruition.com

ALL RIGHTS RESERVED
PRINTED IN THE U.S.A.

DEDICATION

To every overcomer who needs hope!

AN OVERCOMERS PRAYER

Father God, I pray for each person reading this book. I know You did not allow them to purchase or receive this book by coincidence, because everything You allow has a purpose! So, Father God, I lay them at Your feet today. I pray that the eyes of the heart of each reader may be enlightened, so they will know what the hope of Your calling is, and what the riches are of the glory of Your inheritance in the saints. May they know the surpassing greatness of Your power toward us who believe. I pray their spiritual ears will open to receive revelation as the words You have inspired in these pages. Father God meet them where they are and bring them into a greater understanding of who You are and why You allow tests and trials in our lives. I pray, in the matchless, mighty name of Jesus Christ, my Lord and Savior, Amen.

CONTENTS

Foreword
Preface 5
Introduction 11
Battered But Not Broken 17
Breathe Again 29
From Shackles to Praises 43
From Shame to Shalom 63
Good Grief: In My Father's Eyes 77
How Hope Helped Heal 89
Imagine Me 97
My Faith and God's Favor 113
Silent Scream 131
Weeping May Endure for a Night 139
Who Me? 153
Won't He Do It? 163
Our Hope 173
Conclusion 179
About the Publisher 181

FOREWORD

As a pastor you never know who will walk through the doors of your church. We don't know the trial and tribulations those who sit in our pews on Sunday mornings have or are facing. We are also unaware of what they've accomplished and have been able to overcome.

The first time I met LaKesha L. Williams she was visiting The Remnant of Hope International Church where I serve as pastor. She was quiet, unassuming, and obviously a student of the Word (based on her diligence in taking notes). She never bragged that she had written several books or discussed the hundreds of conferences she has both hosted and served as a keynote speaker. No, she listened, asked questions, and volunteered to serve.

Since that first encounter, LaKesha has become a faithful member of our church, stepping up to serve in any capacity required. She has filled our church with laughter, blessed us with her gift of book publishing, and hosted us at her home. More importantly, LaKesha has shared her testimony. A testimony of triumph and strength, one that requires both courage and fearlessness to reveal.

Her testimony, like that of the women she has gathered for this book, **Hope for the Overcomers Soul**, is real, raw, and relevant. It is undeniably transparent!

What you are about to read is a reminder that life is not happening to you, it's happening for you. Faced with life's challenges; the ugliness of abuse, the fear of not being enough, employment and health issues, the women featured in these testimonies emerge delivered, better (not bitter), and the overcomer in their story changed from victim to victorious. More importantly, our God, the Lord Jesus Christ shines brilliantly as the hero in their lives. He single-handedly pulls them from the dark places and lifts them to triumph in a way only God can.

God's glory, so well expressed in these pages, stands to serve notice to us, the readers, that He is still in the life-saving business. He is still capable and will bring us out! He is a God who rescues! He is indeed Alpha and Omega, the Author and the Finisher, the Way Maker, and the heart Fixer. If you don't know this God, you'll meet Him through the riveting stories of these women. **Hope for the Overcomers Soul** is a soul lifting reminder of the true power of God!

LAKESHA L. WILLIAMS

Margo Gross

About Pastor Margo Gross

Pastor Margo M. Gross was born in Washington, DC and now resides in southern Maryland with her husband and two daughters. Margo is a product of both the District of Columbia and the Calvert County Public School systems. After graduating she earned a Bachelor of Science Degree from the University of Maryland Eastern Shore and a Master of Arts in Teaching from Trinity Washington University. She is a member of Alpha Kappa Alpha Sorority Incorporated and Fierce Ladies Achieving Ministry and Entrepreneurial Success (F.L.A.M.E.S). Pastor Margo is an Amazon bestselling author of **The Push** a 120-day devotional designed to push you into purpose.

Margo has been an educator in the public-school system in the Washington Metropolitan areas and suburbs for almost 20 years. She has won numerous awards in the educational arena including Calvert County Teacher of the Year and Outstanding Educator from the Concerned Black Women of Calvert County. Mrs. Gross is currently a school administrator and is pursuing her PhD in Educational Leadership.

Margo's passion for education is only exceeded by her love for ministry. Pastor Gross has been a minister of the gospel for twenty years. As the Senior Pastor of The Remnant of Hope International Church in Maryland, Pastor Gross seeks to challenge people to live better, equip them to disciple, and

HOPE FOR THE OVERCOMERS SOUL

make a positive impact in the community she serves. Her ministry gift has taken her around the country as well as Trinidad in both educational and ministerial arenas. In addition to her church service, Margo Gross is the founder of Margo Medina Ministries which provides mentorship and motivation through her life-changing PUSH series and gives back to the Community through the R.O.C.K. - (Random Occasions of Care and Kindness) Outreach. Pastor Gross is known for her hands-on approach to leadership development, her transparent delivery of God's word, and her anointing to impart revelation to those who struggle to understand God's word. Pastor Gross is committed to fulfilling God's purpose in her life by empowering and inspiring others to desire a personal relationship with Jesus. It is Pastor Gross's desire to change lives through the word of God and she does so with humility, compassion, and integrity.

For bookings please email: margomedina@verizon.net
Follow Pastor Gross on Facebook @Margo Medina Ministries
& Instagram @Margo_Medina

PREFACE

I am honored that you are reading this book right now. I am even more honored that you have made the choice to take this journey with us. This book is the next installment in the Born Overcomers Series. I want to take a moment to talk about how these books came about.

I was nearing my 29th birthday when I found myself thinking about my life and recalling all I've been through. As people, places, things, events, and experiences flashed through my mind I thought, "Man, that would be a pretty interesting book to read," but I had no clue how to write a book or where to start, so, I started a blog. I had a small following, but I still felt the urge to write a book though I hadn't followed through at that time. About a year passed, and I began seeing a therapist to heal some unresolved issues. These therapy sessions helped me realize a lot about myself, all God had done in my life and all God wanted to do through my life. With the encouragement of my therapist and these discoveries, I finally began writing the book.

HOPE FOR THE OVERCOMERS SOUL

In the beginning, the title was **The Promise**, and I planned on guiding readers through four steps (the pain, the process, the purpose, and the promise) that would lead to discovering your purpose in life and accepting the promise and call God had for your life. I wrote one chapter and was stuck for six months. No new ideas were flowing. I was so frustrated because I knew God called me to write a book, but I couldn't figure out why I was hitting a stumbling block. I had begun sharing my testimony on Social Media, so why was it so hard to write? Little did I know God had other plans for how this book was going to come about and all that would be connected to it.

January 31, 2014, my employment status changed, from gainfully employed to unemployed. God revealed to me then that there was so much more He wanted me to do in this life than just work in Information Technology. This caused me to begin seeking Him to figure out what my next step was. Between February and May of 2014, God continuously revealed things to me and confirmed things in my spirit about how He wanted me to share my testimony and be an encouragement to His people.

One day, I was meeting with Kelley Perry, who is one of the best business coaches in the game. Although we were getting to know each other and talking about our businesses, she inspired me to finish what I'd started months ago. A fire was ignited. Later that day, I went to the library to spend some time with God, and to seek Him about His purpose for my life.

LAKESHA L. WILLIAMS

On that Monday, June 2, 2014, God birthed the first book.

I was praying and asking God, "What is it that You want people to feel or take away from this book?" God revealed to me that all I've witnessed, all I've endured and all I've overcome could be used as tools to inspire, encourage and impact others. The foundation of why I share my testimony has always been Revelation 12:11 (KJV), which says, "And they overcame him by the blood of the Lamb, and by the word of their testimony, and they loved not their lives unto the death." From this scripture I began to search and cross-reference scriptures, searching for a different title for the book because I was no longer feeling **The Promise**.

At first, I came up with **We Shall Overcome**, but that just didn't resonate. I continued searching the Bible and reading the reference scriptures attached to Revelation 12:11. The next title I thought of was **The Blood of the Lamb**, but that one did not click in my spirit either because I felt it didn't fit a book about a person's testimony. So, I continued searching and I came across Psalms 139:16 (NLT) which says, "You saw me before I was born. Every day of my life was recorded in Your book. Every moment was laid out before a single day had passed."

This scripture struck me, and I kept reading it repeatedly until this came to me, "If God knew me before I was born, then He must've known all I would endure in life, which means He equipped me, and even built me to overcome everything I would experience before the foundation of the world.

HOPE FOR THE OVERCOMERS SOUL

Therefore, I was Born to Overcome!" With that epiphany, I discovered the title of the first book: **Born Overcomers**!

From that moment on God began revealing things to me about the book and what He wanted me to do. He showed me "Born Overcomers" was going to be more than just a book. All of this happened on Monday, June 2, 2014.

I was sharing how God had given me the book title with a close friend on Wednesday, June 4, 2014, and she mentioned something about a conference, and that same day I began looking for venues for the 1st Annual Born Overcomers Conference. I also developed a website and filed for incorporation with the State of Maryland for Born Overcomers Inc. By the end of the week, Born Overcomers had developed a following, I had a team on board to help me and we decided on a location to hold the first conference.

As I write this, it is now October 2018, and it has been four years, four months and 26 days since God birth Born Overcomers. I have written one book, five devotionals, co-authored an anthology with actress and comedian Kim Coles and organized one collaboration with five amazing women. God has allowed Born Overcomers Inc. to become a recognized non-profit organization that holds annual conferences, monthly testimony parties and provides outreach in the community.

On March of 2018, I was seeking God about what was next, and He downloaded the book you hold in your hands today.

LAKESHA L. WILLIAMS

This book is sort of like Chicken Soup for the Overcomers Soul inspired by true events that I have overcome along with testimonies from eleven amazing women who have also overcome some of life's toughest challenges.

I am grateful to God for using me to birth this ministry and this new book. I pray that you're encouraged by what you read. The purpose of this book is to awaken an awareness inside of you. An awareness that you were born with what you need to overcome all you may face in this life. Think of this book as a guide or compass of sorts, whose purpose is to get you to begin thinking differently about how you see life's challenges, how you react to them and how you can use what you experience in life to bring fame and glory to God. After reading this book, I pray, you will feel hope! I pray you will feel inspired to endure, overcome and live through life's tests and trials.

Seek God as you read this book, ask Him to reveal areas in your life where you feel like you are not overcoming. Search and memorize scriptures related to those areas and earnestly seek to overcome them.

NEVER FORGET, YOU WERE BORN TO OVERCOME!

INTRODUCTION

It will lead to an opportunity for your testimony.
Luke 21:13

Psalm 22:22 says, "I will tell of Your name to my brethren; In the midst of the assembly I will praise You." David would praise God in the assembly because his private deliverance deserved a public testimony. God wonderfully delivers us in the quiet moments when we are hurting, and we must be prepared to offer public praise for His care.

In the pages that follow, you will read the testimonies of twelve amazing women who endured some of the hardest tests and emerged triumphantly. These women are simply honoring the Lord by bearing witness to His work in their lives.

The Lord commends sharing testimonies throughout His Word, particularly in the Psalms. We continually read of the Psalmist promising to tell of the greatness of the Lord *"in the midst of the congregation."* Often, he asks the Lord to deliver him so that he can testify of God's salvation.

The Bible is filled with the most powerful stories we will ever read or hear, but it isn't just a storybook! It is God's testimony to each of us. Now we are all part of God's story. If you have never accepted Jesus Christ as your personal Savior, you are the reason that He sent His Only Begotten Son to Calvary over 2000 years ago! If you are a believer, then you are also a part of God's story. As Christians we are to repeat the story of God's love to others who need to hear it. That includes the nations around the world, the neighbor across the street and every person like you who will read this book.

And the life was manifested, and we have seen and testify and proclaim to you the eternal life, which was with the Father and was manifested to us — what we have seen and heard we proclaim to you also, so that you too may have fellowship with us; and indeed our fellowship is with the Father, and with His Son Jesus Christ.
First John 1:2-3

In this passage we find that John, who walked with Jesus, was now sharing that story with his readers. He was testifying, announcing the Good News of Jesus to those who would listen.

Did you catch the word, "testify"? I grew up watching a lot of TV, crime dramas in particular. With most there is always bound to be a courtroom scene where someone is being sworn in. If I heard the swearing in of a witness once, I heard it 100 times. *"Do you solemnly swear that the testimony that you are about to give is the truth and nothing but the truth, so help you God?"* What does this tell us? That I watched too much TV? Yes, but it tells us something about giving a testimony. We are to tell the truth!

There is something else we need to understand about a testimony. It is about what we know to be the truth . . . not what we think or what we have heard. It is all about what we know! That's exactly what God expects from each of His followers - to simply share what we know - to testify to others of what God has done in our lives; to what we have seen Him do in our lives. We don't have to have the Bible memorized or be able to answer every question that someone might have about God. We only have to be willing to share the story of what God did in our lives!

During His time on earth that's exactly what happened. Jesus would work in someone's life and they would simply share that story with others.

In the New Testament, the Gospels and the Book of Acts provide us with many examples of men and women who testify about what Jesus has done for them. Here are a few:

When Jesus healed the blind man:

So, a second time they called the man who had been blind, and said to him, "Give glory to God; we know that this man is a sinner." He then answered, "Whether He is a sinner, I do

HOPE FOR THE OVERCOMERS SOUL

not know; one thing I do know, that though I was blind, now I see."
John 9:24-25

By now the man who was blind had heard the same questions over and over by the Pharisees. He did not know how or why he was healed, but he knew that his life had been miraculously changed, and he was not afraid to tell the truth. You don't need to know all the answers in order to share Christ with others. It is important to tell how He has changed your life. Then trust that God will use your words to help others believe in Him too!

When Jesus forgave the Samaritan woman:

Come, see a man who told me all the things that I have done; this is not the Christ, is it?
John 4:29

And they were saying to the woman, "It is no longer because of what you said that we believe, for we have heard for ourselves and know that this One is indeed the Savior of the world."
John 4:42

The disciples were simply ordinary men who told people the extraordinary story of Jesus working in their lives. That was what Jesus wanted them to do, it's what He wants us, to do and it's what you will find in the pages that follow!

LAKESHA L. WILLIAMS

And you will testify also, because you have been with Me from the beginning.
John 15:27

The saints in Revelation 12:10-11 are said to have overcome Satan *"by the blood of the Lamb and by the word of their testimony."* Whatever the exact nature of this testimony, we know they were publicly identifying with Jesus Christ despite the opposition of Satan.

A principle emerges across the pages of Scripture: one of God's design in saving us is that we will, in turn, honor Him by sharing our testimony with others.

The world needs Christians who will not be afraid to live their faith and share their testimony. The Lord commanded us to go into all the world and preach the gospel. We will not be able to do that unless we realize the power and importance of our testimony.

Come and hear, all who fear God, and I will tell of what He has done for my soul.
Psalm 66:16

Our prayer is that, in the testimonies on the pages that follow, you will be inspired, encouraged and filled with hope to not just overcome your current tests and trials but to have the courage to share with others what the Lord has done for your soul.

BATTERED BUT NOT BROKEN

Sitting across from my companion in a courtroom in front of a judge, wasn't how I pictured our love story would be. I never thought it would end. No one goes into a relationship or marriage looking to be abused.

Be completely humble and gentle; be patient, bearing with one another.
Ephesians 42:3

For me, having to get a protective order on someone who professed to love me was necessary to protect my life. How many times have we looked on the news and heard that a woman was killed by her husband or boyfriend? The neighbors and sometimes other family members say they never knew anything was wrong in that marriage or relationship until it was too late to help.

BATTERED BUT NOT BROKEN

For my marriage, the red flags and the writing were on the wall. When dealing with a spouse or companion with an unstable mind, it's literally like walking on eggshells daily. But on the day that my companion was ordered to leave our home, he drove off in the last car that remained of the three that he had totaled. I was left with no transportation, but at least I had my life. The day before that, he made his ideas and thoughts apparent. As I walked over to get my nightgown from the top dresser drawer, I saw three bullets sitting on our dresser. That night, I knew what they meant. Just minutes prior to that, he had been accusing me of cheating for the 10,000th time. Even I was shocked! I quickly snapped a picture of the bullets and sent it to my mom and my older son just in case something happened to me.

Throughout our relationship, I would often ask God to dispatch angels to protect my children and I because there was an uneasiness that seemed to enter with him every day.

Let's rewind to what occurred two months prior to this incident. I had decided to sleep in another room. I refused to sleep in a bed beside him because that was where the accusations and his aggressive behavior occurred. In the intimate space that God created for married couples to express their love, I felt violated. I didn't feel safe in that space because so much pain was there in between those sheets.

There had been occasions in which he had pleasured himself on my back as I slept, leaving my night gown soiled. The mental and emotional scars of abuse are sometimes far worse than the physical scars/bruises. To be sexually exploited in that way was so demeaning and I felt completely violated and disrespected by a man who said he loved me more than life. I often wondered how anyone could love someone he didn't even respect as a person. The exhibition of disrespect hit me to my core. What happened to the loving and protective gentleman who helped me to escape the previous relationship that was so abusive? Where was the knight in shining armor who prayed with me at night before we decided to make the formal commitment? This man allowed his monster to lay dormant until I was all in.

You see, after committing to him, I learned that he didn't trust anyone, so I was always a suspect or under the microscope to the point of his inspection of my underwear and clothes daily. Six months into our commitment, he threatened to kill me if he caught me with my ex-boyfriend. Then within seconds of making that daunting statement, things shifted in his mind and he began acting like he had actually caught me with my ex-boyfriend and he started acting out aggressively towards me. That is an example of his delusional thinking that I could not bring him out of. That was the first incident in which I called my family to assist and rescue me. The incidents that followed were just as bizarre!

In hindsight, he had displayed this paranoid/delusional behavior before we started dating, but I dismissed it as my being pessimistic! What further fueled his suspicion was that we lived in two different cities. I had not found a job in the city where he resided, and he was a student in a field that was in demand. You see I had decided to commit based upon his potential and unfortunately, I didn't get to see that potential manifest in our time together. You see this man was more committed to his drug of choice than he was committed to providing and contributing to the household financially.

Husbands love your wives just as Christ loved the church and gave Himself up for her.
Ephesians 5:25

The lesson to learn here is If a man isn't working before you commit to him, how will you know if he has a work ethic? Make sure that he has the attributes and character of Boaz. Boaz made sure Ruth was taken care of. In addition to him not being able to contribute financially, there were bizarre incidents that followed that would have spooked the bravest woman. After a long day at work, a neighborhood child noticed that a man was camped out on the side of our house one evening and he alerted someone to tell me. As I exited the house to investigate, I observed that it was my companion as he was running across the lawn in the backyard. Needless to say, he was issued a few choice words as I told him that his behavior was as just bizarre! He said it was a joke, but it certainly was not a laughing matter to me or my loved ones. According to him, all his insecurities were there because we lived apart.

The next incident occurred one night at about 3:00 a.m. He drove to my house which was two hours away and stood there and watched me sleep for five minutes and then he drove back home. It freaked my family and I out because they saw him when he entered at 3:00 a.m. and when he exited. A year later, I moved to his city and we lived in the same house. This time, I was awakened out of my sleep one night at around 2:00 a.m. with him accusing me of texting someone as I laid right next to him. He argued me down. How do you convince a person that you were asleep when they are delusional? From that day forward, I never felt comfortable lying in bed next to him. I often wondered how he could love someone he didn't even respect as a person. That issue was something from his past that was unresolved, and I was not willing to accept his disrespect and mistreatment.

Never settle and expose yourself to abuse to save face. God only wants the best for us, so know your worth. God will help you to create a plan of escape. He will also help you to find a healthy support system to aid in your decision or He will open doors. The home is a sacred place and nothing or nobody is worth sacrificing your safety, life, and peace. Peace is a gift from God and I refused to allow my companion to take it from me. I had battled enough in the past to know that whatever God delivers us from in our past, it is not meant to be picked up again! You have to rebuke that thing and send it back to the pits of hell in the name of Jesus.

Stay focused and only look back to be grateful for where God has brought you from and use it as a testimony to help others. Just as I asked God to dispatch His angels to guide and protect me while in an abusive relationship, I also ask God to send His ministering angels to help you in whatever you do. Always allow God to be your co-pilot. Just know nothing is too big or small for God! We just have to learn to trust Him and His word and know that He loves us even when we are in unfavorable situations. Those situations can and will be used later to minister to someone who feels alone in their situation.

Toxic relationships are merely distractions to get you off the path to your destiny. The devil peaks into our future and he knows what we can become and accomplish if we remain focused. Thank God in advance for the open and closed doors because He knows what you need. Let great pain and trials give birth to your passion. Your passion may fuel and motivate others to pursue their goals/dreams. Realize also that during the climb to success, obstacles will come, but we must develop the tenacity to overcome them or see through them in spite of them. You may be one step away from your breakthrough, so push. God has blessings stored up for His people, but we just have to persevere even when we feel like giving up.

Just realize that only you can create your legacy, and you are the determining factor in whether your family elevates. You determine what your legacy will be or if you are remembered or forgotten by future generations. You set the bar that can motivate others to excel. There's nothing wrong with sharing your testimony with your family and others. People often see you on your pedestal, but they will not know about the challenges of the climb to the pedestal if you don't share them. Sometimes people feel alone on their climb to success, so your testimony will help others to identify with them and relate.

Life is real, so offering encouraging words to others could be a ministry in and of itself. Reflecting on what and where God has brought you through and from can be so humbling. There are plenty of individuals who have lost their minds during challenging times but thank God that He preserved them even if they do have a few battle scars. They are still here and that's worth a praise to God.

I can recall a time in my life when I barely had food, electricity, water, and shelter. We often complain about having to pay for these things, but at least we have the resources to pay for them. When you get frustrated and discouraged about paying bills, think of what it felt like to not have a job and how terrible it was if you had to have children depending on you, though you could barely provide for them. God got you through that!

How about that car with a few flaws but it runs? Flashback to when you didn't have your own car or when you couldn't drive it because it needed to be repaired. Don't take so much for granted. Let's even flashback to what it was like when you were single if you are married. You had to bring in your own groceries, wash your own car and cut your own grass. Be thankful for a man but make it mandatory that he has a job or income. Don't settle! Men are intended to be providers so if your man is not, then what truly is his role in your life? Some men want to be taken care of financially, but make sure they bring something to the table and don't ignore any of the red flags please. Make sure that he has maintained a steady job and evaluate his work history. Ignoring the red flags, can cost you in the long run and can lead to you losing a great deal of what you had before you met him. Evaluate if he truly is an asset or liability to your life, goals, and future.

No one's perfect but don't risk it all for love or because of desperation. Rewind, remember how I ignored all the signs and red flags and I almost lost my life? True love will happen, and things will line up if you will put your trust in God! Don't leap into a relationship because you feel like you are getting older because it could come at a huge cost! When you are in an unhealthy situation it impacts your whole family. Those are years that you can't get back in your children's lives. Your children deserve the best life you can give them so don't settle.

Psalms 139:14 says, *I praise you because I am fearfully and wonderfully made"* so there is no room for settling.

I know and recognize that I was blessed while in my marriage because within the pain of it, my baby was born. In two years, I have co-authored two books and now, I am the host of my own radio show, *Inspire & Uplift Radio Show with LaShonda Oates Milsap*. In my books I shared my testimonies of how I have survived numerous traumas and now in my job, I am able to help and inspire others to defy obstacles. On my radio show, some of the professionals and featured entrepreneurs share their testimonies of how they overcame child sexual abuse, poor self-esteem issues, grief/loss, and other issues. Through my life experiences, I can now encourage others to excel inspire of their challenges.

About LaShonda Oates Milsap

LaShonda Oates Milsap is the daughter of Freeman and Ella Oates of Fayetteville, NC. LaShonda is a woman who has a heart for helping and motivating others. She is a mother, daughter, sister, and social worker, and she finds each role to be greatly rewarding in their own unique way. LaShonda is an innovative thinker and uses her experiences to advocate and motivate others. Her aspiration is to utilize her gifts and talents to touch others' lives, so they can reach their potential and bless the lives of others.

In addition, LaShonda holds a bachelor's degree from Fayetteville State University and master's degree in Social Work from Smith College in Northampton, Massachusetts. Her hobbies include: hiking, traveling, learning about different cultures, and attending sporting events. She regularly attends John Wesley United Methodist and is a member of Delta Sigma Theta Sorority, Incorporated. She has four sons: Cameran, Mitchell, Derrick, and Steven.

LaShonda has co-authored two books, God is Able, Our Journey and Be A Voice. She is the host of her own online radio show, **Inspire & Uplift Radio Show with LaShonda Oates Milsap** and its purpose is to inspire others to pursue their goals, dreams, and aspirations by having featured guests to share their testimonies of how they succeeded.

LASHONDA OATES MILSAP

Contact

Website: lashondaomilsap@weebly.com
Radio show: Inspire & Uplift Radio Show with LaShonda Oates Milsap on Streaminginspiration.net/?page_id=27571
Facebook: LaShonda Oates Milsap
Instagram: msoatesdst8
Snapchat: lmilsap1
YouTube: LaShonda Oates Milsap, Author

LaShonda's Acknowledgements

I would like to thank God for the opportunity to share my testimony to bless and encourage others! I would like to dedicate this book collaboration to my late father, Freeman Oates, my mom, Ella Mae Oates Bohannon, and to my sons: Cameran and Mitchell Oates. I would like to also like to dedicate my chapter to victims of domestic violence and their families. God is truly awesome!

BREATHE AGAIN

For as many years as I can remember, each day of my life has included some sort of mini adventure. Whether it's the routine trip to the store, engaging with the patients at the office, something at church, or something involving my household members: there is always a story to write about at the end of the day.

I recall during my first year of college, not long after having turned 17, I had what I'd say was a pretty scary episode. I attended Howard University and was a Washington, DC resident, so I didn't stay on campus. I'd commute using Metro, both the bus and the rail. I'd get off at the Shaw-Howard Metro Station on 7th St. N.W., between R and S streets. Depending on how I felt on a given day, I'd either catch the 70 bus up the hill or I'd walk.

One day in particular when I had chosen to walk, I had a really difficult time catching my breath after getting to campus at the top of the hill. It was as if I'd run a marathon,

BREATHE AGAIN

but I hadn't run at all. During that time, I had otherwise been in pretty good shape: especially since my first class of the day in my first semester was fitness. Warm-ups were us running around the track and we'd engage in other exercises to enhance our health. I wasn't originally a fan of the course because our professor was kind, but he was no-nonsense. I eventually developed an appreciation for the course because I noticed the benefits. Years later, I'd come to find out that the same fitness instructor had once been my husband's wrestling coach. I digress. Let's get back to the day where I felt less than fit. Because of the fitness class, I'd been accustomed to walking and running, but on this day, walking posed a challenge for me and it felt like a truck was sitting on my chest. The more I walked, the weaker I got, and the more I panted. I finally made my way to what had been one of my favorite spots on campus, *The Punchout*.

I didn't stay on campus, and I had some days where I had breaks in between classes that would be hours long, so I spent quite a bit of time at *The Punchout*. Located in Howard University's Blackburn Center, *The Punchout* is a popular dining spot on campus. I had no job, but I had a few dollars a day and I'd either enjoy an omelet from *The Punchout* or I'd grab a Jamaican beef patty and coco bread from a nearby food truck and then take it to *The Punchout* to enjoy. I would say that I'd utilize the breaks in between classes to study, but that wouldn't be true. Since it was a favorite and familiar place, I decided to go there to try to collect myself when I had this difficult breathing episode.

DANIELLE N. HALL

I sat down for a moment and when I felt like my breathing calmed down enough, I recall mustering up enough strength to order a ham and cheese omelet. Listen, I know breathing is important, but so is food, right? I received my omelet and sat back down. It literally took me about 2 hours to get myself together enough to breathe near normal. Now one may beg the question: *"Why didn't you seek help?"* or *"Why didn't anyone help you?"* Honestly, I didn't see many people and the ones who I did see probably didn't think much of it. I had chest heaviness and not really an audible wheeze. As to the question of why I didn't seek help, the answer is easy: I'm Bobby's daughter.

Up until his transition in December 2017, my dad Robert Brock-Smith, Sr., (who I affectionately called Bobby) was a fighter. He endured a lot of pain and discomfort over the years. He had suffered with gout and, in his later years, rheumatoid arthritis. When Dad's gout would flare up, he'd resort to his special blend of herbs that he would use to create his own capsules at home. He'd be so proud of his concoction and its effectiveness. His herbal blends would work, but Dad wasn't consistent. Nevertheless, he wasn't the "go to the doctor" or hospital type. It may be in part because of his experience as a medic in the army. Dad even kept all kinds of medical supplies and equipment in the house. Let's just say that the whole apple not falling too far from the tree thought may have some validity.

By the time I had enrolled at Howard University, I'd already spent the past 3 summers as a teen working in a hospital as a

BREATHE AGAIN

benefit of being a part of the Health and Human Services Academy at Eastern Senior High School in Washington, DC. I was afforded the privilege of working in the Family Health Clinic at Hadley Memorial Hospital (now Bridgepoint). I initially aspired to become a pediatrician specializing in neonatology and this hospital was closest to me, however, there was no pediatric ward. Providers at the clinic included internal medicine physicians, a gynecologist, a pediatrician, and more. I was always intrigued by the human body since childhood. Growing up, I studied the Family Medical Guide we had at home. Much like Dad, if it was a problem I could fix on my own, I would try to do just that. I observed and learned so much and was all about applying what I did know. This, in no way, is meant to downplay the schooling, experience, and expertise of those who have worked so hard in preparation of providing quality services that enhance and preserve life. I, too, was on that track at Howard as I was pursuing a Master's Degree in Physical Therapy.

As I sat in *The Punchout* that day, my resolution to this breathing challenge was to breathe. I had to think fast and that was the thought that came to mind. I'm sure it sounds crazy, but I sat still and took slow breaths and repeated this process until my breathing calmed down and became less laborsome. Eventually, I was relieved. It was an unforgettable moment. More moments would follow in the future.

Fast forward a few years to a different location. Picture it... DC....1999. It was about summertime and the temperatures were a little on the high side. I've never been a fan of the heat, but the way my job was set up, outdoor activities were a part of the program. I mentioned having been intrigued by the human body at an early age. The truth is, since childhood, I was often conflicted between the thoughts of growing up and becoming a doctor or a teacher. After having some financial challenges with loans for school not coming in on time, I chose to work in a child care center. I was at one center for just a few months and then I secured employment at Big Mama's Children's Center in 1998. The center is accredited and services children from ages 6 weeks to 12 years of age. The children, who have the privilege of receiving care at Big Mama's Children's Center, are in an environment which supports development emotionally, physically, socially, and cognitively. Unlike the experience I had at the first child care center, Big Mama's provided balance and structure.

In 1999, new playground equipment had been installed on the center's grounds. For surfacing purposes, wood chips were utilized to help protect children from injuries. A safe and healthy learning environment is paramount when it comes to childcare. The children were excited about the new playground equipment and so was I. There was one problem. Apparently, I was extremely allergic to the wood chips. I had a severe allergic reaction. I sneezed repeatedly, my eyes were running, and that difficult breathing surfaced again. This time, going to the hospital didn't seem like something to discount. I went to the emergency room and, at the age of 20, I was diagnosed with asthma. As I thought about other episodes that were similar, I concluded that asthma was probably an issue I had dealt with for longer than I thought. This could be because growing up both of my parents were cigarette smokers.

According to the Center for Disease Control (CDC) "Tobacco use remains the single largest preventable cause of death and disease in the United States. Cigarette smoking kills more than 480,000 Americans each year, with more than 41,000 of these deaths from exposure to secondhand smoke. In addition, smoking-related illness in the United States costs more than $300 billion a year, including nearly $170 billion in direct medical care for adults and $156 billion in lost productivity." I'm grateful to say that both of my parents quit smoking and neither developed lung cancer. Unfortunately, I did become afflicted by asthma. Again, according to the CDC, "Secondhand smoke contains more than 7,000 chemicals. Hundreds are toxic and about 70 can cause cancer. Secondhand smoke causes numerous health problems in infants and children, including more frequent and severe asthma attacks, respiratory infections, ear infections, and sudden infant death syndrome (SIDS)."

In the years to follow, the list of things that would trigger these asthma symptoms for me would increase. After showering I'd have to quickly cover my chest area because exposure to cool air would exacerbate symptoms. Some household cleaning products became a problem for me as well. Pine Sol was often used at Big Mama's and I discovered that my body would negatively respond to breathing it in. Without having been officially tested, I knew that dust, mold, and mildew were problematic for me as well. In another memorable episode, I recall moving a stand that held my stereo component and other items. For some reason, mildew had developed on the wall behind the stand and when it was exposed after moving the stand, I found that my chest began to tighten, and breathing became more of a struggle. This episode was before I was diagnosed with asthma. The way I recovered from this episode was the same way I recovered from the incident at Howard -- slow, deep breaths.

The cool, damp air was another trigger for me. I'd have to make sure my chest and neck were covered when exposed to the cool, damp air outside. Otherwise, I'd have to utilize my rescue inhaler. Overexertion and exercise like walking uphill would bring on asthma symptoms.

Despite suffering with this newfound condition, I successfully carried and delivered my first child in December 1999. During the pregnancy, I'd walk often, both while working at Big Mama's and after work hours. Ultimately, I believe the walking helped me to maintain a healthy pregnancy weight. I gave birth to my one and only girl who came in weighing a whopping 5 lbs. 13 oz. If you detected the sarcasm there, then I know I have your attention. She was small, but she was strong. When she was 1 month old, she contracted a respiratory virus that required her to be hospitalized. Her symptoms were a dry, whooping cough and what was an evident struggle to catch her breath. She was diagnosed with RSV (respiratory syncytial virus) which *"is the most common cause of bronchiolitis (inflammation of the small airways in the*

BREATHE AGAIN

lung) and pneumonia (infection of the lungs) in children younger than 1 year of age" according to the CDC. She was in the hospital for 4 days and it was awhile before I could hold her there because she was under an oxygen tent that was sustaining her. It was hard enough dealing with breathing problems of my own, but to see my wee one suffering was heartbreaking because there wasn't much I could do for her and I felt helpless at times. The months progressed, and we made several trips to the emergency room where she would have to be treated for difficulty breathing. Many long nights were spent at Children's Hospital. She was also eventually diagnosed with asthma.

In 2002, I was still employed at Big Mama's and I became pregnant with my 2nd child, my first son. The pregnancy presented challenges and all health issues I had previously dealt with were amplified. It became a growing challenge to remain at Big Mama's and I soon found myself at home trying to adjust to these changes in my body. I would blackout, I couldn't keep food down, and my sense of sound was amplified triggering vertigo attacks. I got past what I thought was the most difficult phase and returned to the other industry I loved so much, healthcare. I joined the administrative team at an ophthalmology practice. It was a low maintenance job, however, I had a difficult pregnancy which required me to be placed on bed rest in my last trimester. I went through a series of things to help prevent and prepare for a premature delivery. I'd begin having contractions pretty early on. I was prescribed a medication called terbutaline. This was supposed to prevent pre-term labor and help me with asthma symptoms simultaneously. Unfortunately, it didn't help the contractions to cease and it made my asthma symptoms worse. I discontinued the medication.

On New Year's Eve at 11:29 pm, I successfully gave birth to my second child, born at 37 weeks like his sister. There was a problem, though. He wasn't breathing and had begun to turn blue. The healthcare staff worked hard and got him to show us the strength of his lungs when he let out a loud cry. Being born at 37 weeks wasn't the only thing he shared in common with his sister. He was also diagnosed at a young age with asthma. A year and a half later I gave birth to my last child, who also arrived at 37 weeks. I'm so happy to say that he did not have to deal with the asthma struggle.

Due to the eldest two children having asthma, we had a nebulizer in the home. Nevertheless, trips to the emergency room became a routine for me during certain times of the year when neither the nebulizer treatments nor the rescue inhaler were enough. I'd have to "go get zapped" as my husband would say. I'd have to have extra nebulizer treatments and get steroids. I'd usually develop bronchitis and would wind up being prescribed an antibiotic to alleviate that problem. This lifestyle became cumbersome, but I didn't let it stop me from faithfully serving in the music ministry at church. I'd sing in spite of the breathing challenges. I was a faithful servant, but my faith still had much room to grow.

In 2013, my husband had experienced a major health crisis. He had a boil which wound up getting infected and consequently caused his kidneys to shut down to a function of only 5%. He pretty much immediately became a dialysis patient receiving treatments three times a week. Additionally, he was diagnosed with pneumonia and had gout in just about every joint. I prayed and prayed and when I would head to the hospital to visit him, I'd listen to two songs on repeat: *"I've Seen Him Do It"* by Kurt Carr and *"Last Say So"* by Kim Rutherford. What he experienced a few months after being on dialysis was nothing short of miraculous. His kidney function improved, and he no longer required dialysis! I was so grateful for this display of God's love and mercy.

When his birthday came around a few months later on February 2, 2014, I remember thanking God so much as I reflected on what his condition had been just months before and here he was celebrating another year, then the epiphany came. I had believed God so much for my husband's healing to manifest, but I hadn't considered the same for myself. It was a Sunday morning and I was preparing for church. I began to believe God for my own healing and I said aloud that I didn't want to take any medicine anymore. By this point I had been taking multiple medications to address asthma and allergy flare ups. I declared by faith that I was asthma free on the morning of February 2, 2014.

I am so excited to say that now, in 2018, I have been medication and symptom free for four and a half years. After having been tried for several years by this exhausting condition, by God's grace I triumphed over it! I overcame that which was causing me to be overcome by it. At least once a week, I use the peak flow meter which was given to me during my emergency room visits. It is used to measure the air flowing in and out of the lungs. It always makes my heart glad when I see that my peak flow rate is higher with no medication than my best was when on several medications. I do not cease to give God thanks for gracing me to overcome this challenge that kept me in the emergency room, that kept me missing days at work, that kept me missing out on certain activities with my children, and that kept me medicated. It is so liberating to have overcome asthma...to be able to BREATHE AGAIN!

What I've learned in my life as a Believer is that it's easy for us to believe God for blessings, healing, breakthrough, and miracles for others. The challenge is when it comes to believing God about our own situation. In my church, the theme this year is: *"I Believe My Faith Makes the Difference"*, and the scriptural foundation is the beginning of Hebrews 11:6 which reads, *"But without faith it is impossible to please Him."* In the case of Asthma vs. Danielle, I'm convinced that I received my healing because my faith made the difference. I sing loud with a voice of triumph because I was once bound and near gagged by asthma! *But thanks be to God, who always leads us in triumph in Christ, and through us spreads and makes evident everywhere the sweet fragrance of the knowledge of Him.* 2 Corinthians 2:14a (AMP). Thank God, I can breathe again!

About Danielle N. Hall

Minister Danielle N. Hall is an advocate for all to recognize and fulfill their divine purpose. She continually seeks opportunities to enlighten, empower, and encourage. She believes a life best-lived is a poured-out life. She is the author of *Dew Drops: Refreshing for the Soul* and the creator of *"Danielle's Place"*: a website where visitors can visit and get food for the soul. Additionally, she is one of many co-authors of the book project, *"She Wouldn't Let Me Fall"*, which was released on March 9th, 2018. Her second solo book, *"Dirty Little Secrets and The Little White Lie"*, is set for its debut at the end of 2018. Danielle is also the founder of V.O.I.C.E. (Victorious Overcomers Inspiring Christian Empowerment) – a ministry that serves women who have been sexually abused. She is a married mother of 3 children and enjoys reading, writing, singing, and aiding others.

Contact

Email: mrsdaniellenhall@yahoo.com
Facebook: @writefrommyhearttoyours
Instagram: @daniellenhall1
Twitter: @DanielleNHall1
Website: daniellenhall.com
To purchase Dew Drops: Refreshing for the Soul use this link: https://www.amazon.com/Dew-Drops-Refreshing-Danielle-Hall/dp/0997948396

Danielle's Acknowledgements

Dedicated in loving memory of my late father, Robert H. Brock-Smith, Sr. Thank you for being the wind beneath my wings to help me fly and just keep going.

To my mother, Cheryl V. Brock-Smith, you are the epitome of strength and the greatest inspiration to give me the courage to overcome.

To my husband Moe and children: Jayla, Maurice, Jr. & Aaron, thank you for allowing me to be myself and to live a life-poured out.

To the visionary of this book, LaKesha L. Williams, thank you for the opportunity to share my testimony and for being a trailblazer for overcomers!

To my Lord and Savior, thank You for giving me a testimony and for allowing me to grow through every life experience.

FROM SHACKLES TO PRAISES

I thought working for Society Association for almost 21 years making a decent salary was all God had for me. I worked my way up the career ladder and was happy at the progress I made over the years. I always went above and beyond my job responsibilities and was noticed by many, so I was happy with the position I was in.

I worked with a great team of employees who I cared about as I did my own family. We all got along very well. I had two supervisors, Bernard and Ivory. Bernard was very easygoing and not hard to get along with. Ivory was an entirely different story. Let's just say that everyone thought of her as being a very evil person. Because I wasn't on her plotting and planning committee I wasn't one of her favorites. Regardless of how I was treated by Ivory, I stayed focused on the job that I was hired to do.

I've often heard that God sometimes talks to you through dreams and I'm a believer that this is true. During staff meetings with Bernard and Ivory, hateful things were said about my staff. One day I couldn't take it any longer, so I spoke up to defend the people who worked hard every day. That night in a dream, I was told that there was a serpent roaming in my office, so I needed to be careful. This dream stuck in my mind for years while working at Society. Each day I would listen to negativity from Ivory, but I tried to stay as far away from her as I could. Some days were harder than others, but I always managed to push through with prayer. I believed that God had something better for me, so I started praying harder and harder each day. I started to pray that God would place me in a position where I would be responsible for myself and I could continue making the same salary. Little did I know that God would do exactly what I asked and prayed for. So, I learned to be specific about what you want and how you want it to happen.

Now let's talk about Myra. Myra was another manager under the same organization. I've heard some horror stories about the type of manager she was, but I didn't concern myself with this and instead kept focusing on my work. I only knew that she was working at Society for a very short time before she was promoted. Actually, she became one of my managers, but I rarely interacted with her.

One day I received an email from Myra asking me to give her a call. Little did I know this call would tremendously change my faith from just believing in God to really depending on Him.

Myra started off by telling me that she wanted me to be her Senior Advisor. She said that she'd heard nothing but great things about me and that she needed someone like me on her team. Myra stated that she's a praying woman and she's been asking God to send her the right people and God sent her to me. At the end of the call, I asked Myra if I could have some time to think about my decision. Her exact words were, "don't think too long because opportunities like this don't come that often to girls of color." I thought that this was an odd response but didn't dwell on it too much. Myra gave me a week to decide if I wanted to take her offer.

I was happy to be offered such a high-level position, but I also wondered why she selected me being that I never had a conversation with her. After the call, I shared the details of the phone call with my husband and kids. Of course, they were happy for me and told me to accept the offer. I immediately told them that I didn't think this offer was from God. They told me that I was overreacting. I kept telling them that I could feel in my spirit that something wasn't right. Most people would be ecstatic about the offer, but I immediately began to feel sad and depressed.

From the time I received the phone call until the time I had to make my decision, I just didn't feel like myself. I started talking to God every day and asking Him to let me know if this was from Him. God kept telling me again and again that this was not from Him. When the day came for me to give Myra my answer, I did something that I thought I would regret for the rest of my life. Even though I knew God told me to say no, I

FROM SHACKLES TO PRAISES

said yes. So here we go.

Several days after I said yes, Myra told me that she actually only wanted me to work with her for a very short time period. She stated that after that time I would have to find another position and office to work in. That was when I learned that Myra tricked me, and she had used God's name in her bag of tricks. After requesting to stay in my position, Myra said that I had no choice and that she had gave my slot to another supervisor coming on board. Because I kept inquiring about remaining in my position, Myra went from telling me how great of an employee I was to how terrible of an employee I was. She went as far as to call me insubordinate and said that I needed to be watched on a daily basis. She also said that she didn't think that I deserved the excellent performance reviews that I received over the years. She told me that she didn't have time for me because she was too high on the career ladder to have time to talk to someone like me. I could not believe how I went from being a high-performing employee to be a terrible one, especially from someone who did not even know me.

Days turned into weeks, weeks turned into months, and months turned into years and I was treated awful. I was so mad at myself because God had given me His answer, but I did not listen. Day by day I became miserable. I could not believe this was happening to me. After all, I was a dedicated employee and worked hard every day and this was the thanks I was getting. After months of going back and forth with Myra, I was removed from my office, told to sit in a corner cubicle, and reassigned to a different manager because Myra decided I was not worth her time. Myra made my working environment a living nightmare by treating me like I was the worst person on earth. I was beyond miserable and started to spend more and more time with God. I never got mad with God because He reminded me that He gave me everything I prayed for. I kept reminding God that I didn't ask for it to happen in such a nasty manner.

Working in such a hostile environment, I found myself in a state of depression and did nothing but cry. Not long before this happened, I had lost my mother-in-law, my Dad, two Aunts, and a cousin all within months from each other. So, I was still grieving the loss of my loved ones and just couldn't digest everything that was going on. One day while at work I received such a hateful email from Myra that it raised my blood pressure to the point where I fell out. Luckily, a co-worker was near and was able to call the nurse. The ambulance arrived and stated that my blood pressure was at a dangerous rate and wanted to take me to the nearest hospital. I refused to go to the hospital and just headed home to weep alone in misery. I made an appointment to see my doctor the next day and he ordered me to take the rest of the week off. I obeyed his orders, but I didn't want to talk to anyone or be around anyone. I was too miserable to tell my family what was going on.

By the grace of God, I had some prayer partners, Darlene and Martha from work who witnessed everything going on. They became my rock, along with God. They would pray with me day and night to keep me uplifted and focused on God. They wouldn't let me give up and always reminded me that God was with me. Their spiritual guidance helped me to slowly let go of the emotional bondage that had me strapped. I thank God for using these mighty women of God because without their encouragement, I don't know how this story would have ended. One weekend while riding home, I had my 7-year-old niece, British, in the back seat and she could tell that I wasn't my usual self. British asked me what was wrong, and I told her that someone had lied to me at work and I was sad. She said just tell the lady "not today boo-boo!" I think this is the first time I laughed since my life was in shambles (at least I thought it was in shambles). When Myra would send me nasty emails, I would say to myself "not today boo-boo!"

Moving forward, I realized that I could not fight this fight on my own, so I hired an attorney. After one month from hiring an attorney I could no longer afford the cost of an attorney after paying out thousands of dollars for little work. Therefore, I found myself fighting the case on my own and depending on my Lord and Savior Jesus Christ. I never stopped talking to Him. I just kept asking God to send me messages so that I'll know it's from Him. One night before work, I had another dream. I was about to walk outside to check the weather for the day. My husband was still upstairs getting dressed. When I opened the door, my front yard was full of white sheep. I was really scared so I hurried and tried to shut the door.

The sheep stopped me from closing the door and said, "He sent us to tell you everything would be alright."

CASSANDRA FOOKS

I asked the sheep who sent them, and they kept saying, "He sent us, He sent us." I started yelling my husband's name, but he couldn't hear me.

The sheep said, "We're not going to hurt you. We just came to tell you what He said."

I started screaming, "No! No! Leave me alone!" In that moment, my husband woke me up and I realized I was dreaming.

I always think about that dream and know it was a voice from God. When I arrived to work in the morning Myra had done things to let me know that she still despised me. When I got home that evening, I decided to attend Bible study at River Baptist Worship Center under the direction of Pastor Marvin. River Baptist was my home church that I've attended for years. I didn't want to go and just wanted to shut out the world, but something kept nagging at me to attend. That evening Pastor Marvin taught about how some setbacks are a setup from God to balance your books. He taught about how God will give you rest and renew your strength. I just sat and listened to the lesson but wasn't ready to receive it. I came home that night, prayed, and cried myself to sleep. My husband became frustrated from seeing me cry day and night and told me to quit. He offered to get another job to help make ends meet but I wasn't ready to give up just yet. I knew that God didn't want me to quit.

I would get discouraged because I didn't think God heard

me but somewhere in my heart I knew that He did. Myra continued to treat me horribly and treated me different than everyone else. Every year before Christmas, the employees would all receive a bonus for their performance. When it was time for my bonus, I never received one. I was upset but not as upset as many would've been. God reminded me that He was still in control, so I just stayed focused on Him. The next day I looked in the mailbox and there was a refund check from our mortgage company saying that we had been paying too much. The letter also stated that our mortgage was going to decrease due to an error made by the mortgage company. Several weeks later I noticed that my paycheck increased due to a raise I had received but was unaware of. I just kept praising God because I knew this was all from Him. I knew this was another sign from Him letting me know that He's got my back. I knew it was God telling me not to worry about a bonus but to stay focused on my biggest bonus which was getting to know Him.

I kept asking God not to forget me. The next morning, I was telecommuting and when I started working there was a tapping at my front door. I looked out the door and there were 3 pretty blue birds tapping at my door. When I opened the door, the birds started talking to me before they flew away. I immediately smiled and said, "Thank you Jesus!" I knew that this was another message from God. The hostile working environment continued at work, but I hung in there. Normally I would defend myself by responding to negative emails from Myra but one day God told me to close my mouth and let Him handle things. Now a sistah started shaking her head and telling God that I needed to defend myself but as the days went by, I began to listen to what God was telling me. I was still miserable, but God never stopped speaking to me.

I was at a point where I just didn't want to attend church anymore, but God wouldn't let me give up. I continued attending church and weekly Bible study because Pastor Marvin's sermons always spoke directly to my situation. Sometimes I wondered if he knew about my situation because he was always right on time. One Sunday I arrived at church feeling angry and really didn't want to be there. Pastor Marvin preached about forgetting what lies behind and stream toward what lies ahead of us. He said that excessive mourning stops God from blessing us with our future. I just sat and listened to every word that he said. Almost every Sunday, I would receive a call from Darlene or Martha and we would share what we learned during Sunday Service. This helped me make it through another day.

As time passed, the stress started to take a toll on me, so I decided to make a visit to my doctor. I was diagnosed with severe depression and my doctor placed me on medication; however, I refused to let the devil win and I didn't take the medication as prescribed. While driving home from the doctor, I was crying uncontrollably. I started telling God that I was tired of dealing with Myra and her nasty ways toward me. I asked God when He was going to show up. In the middle of my breakdown while driving, out of nowhere my car started talking to me. It kept repeating "Your passenger

FROM SHACKLES TO PRAISES

seatbelt is unbuckled" over and over again. I started saying that I don't have a passenger, but the voice got louder and louder. I've never heard my car talk, so I was a bit startled. My purse was in the passenger seat, so I started moving my purse around, but the voice kept getting louder. At that moment, God let me know that this was His voice and He was right there by my side. I immediately wiped my tears and went into praising Him. I wanted to get out of the car and just do a praise dance right in the middle of the street. I smiled for the rest of the day knowing that I had a personal interaction with God.

The next Sunday, Pastor Marvin preached about how when negative things happen it's not the end of your destiny but it's actually the start of your destiny. Pastor said that when God puts a dream in your heart in tough times you have to remember your dream. He reminded us to let Him fight and don't get bitter because it's a detour on the way to your destiny. He reminded the congregation that the favor of God is defeating your enemies. After hearing this I kept thinking about the dream with the sheep and I immediately started to think on a different level.

Myra still continued to treat me bad, but I was able to deal with it a little better. I learned to ignore her, smile more, keep my mouth shut, and work on myself. In Pastor Marvin's sermons he let me know that I always have access to God, so I kept talking to Him and never stopped. Sometimes I would wake up in the wee hours of the morning and just talk to Him until I was satisfied that He heard me. God kept reminding me that I was still human and even though I turned it over to Him, it was still alright to cry. One day while home alone, I was upstairs praying and crying out to Him. I asked God to reveal Himself once again to let me know that He didn't forget about me. In an instant, I heard a door loudly open and close, so I thought it was my husband coming home from work early. I hurried and wiped my tears because I didn't want him to see me crying nor did I want him to think that I was taking back what I had turned over to God. The odd thing is that my house alarm was on, but it never went off. Usually something like this would've startled me but somehow, I knew it was God showing up again. I crept downstairs and looked around, but I didn't see anyone. I just started thanking God for His grace and mercy.

As time went by, I continued my daily prayers and started trusting and believing in God more and more. Sunday after Sunday, Pastor Marvin preached sermons that helped me make it through this miserable time in my life. Whenever I would need comfort or an answer from God, he would always remind me of how He sent His sheep. God reminded me of John 10:25-29 *Jesus answered them, I told you, and ye believe not: the works that I do in my Father's name, they bear witness of me. But ye believe not, because ye are not of my sheep, as I said unto you. My sheep hear my voice, and I know them, and they follow Me: And I give unto them eternal life; and they shall never perish, neither shall any man pluck them out of My hand.*

The harassment at work continued but I learned to keep my

FROM SHACKLES TO PRAISES

mouth shut and let God work it out. I watched Myra treat others just as bad as she treated me, but I kept pleading the Blood of Jesus. Myra was sure to let the staff know that she was in charge. Myra would walk by my desk, speak to other staff members, and turn her nose up at me but I learned to laugh and just smile. The leadership at Society was changing so new managers were coming on board. God kept reminding me that He was going to remove those who meant me no good from my life. Honestly, I wanted Him to remove me from having any contact with Myra, but she still treated me like I was beneath her. As time went by, there were rumors that Myra may be leaving Society for unknown reasons. I didn't get involved with the rumors and kept obeying and talking to God. I kept attending church and Bible study and obeying His Word.

One Sunday Pastor Marvin preached about how God is going to straighten me out, my places out, and my haters out. One thing he said was to start speaking to your situation and God will act on your behalf. He talked about speaking boldly and getting freedom from fools. So, I started speaking more and more to my situation and asking God to move but in His time. I kept asking God to use me how He wants to use me. I knew it was time for a change. God spoke to me and said that what certain people meant for evil He meant for my good. Pastor Marvin announced that the church needed more teachers for children's Bible study. I love kids and I've always wanted to work with children, but I've always been a behind the scenes person. I prayed about it and I finally volunteered to teach children's Bible study.

But there was more that God wanted from me. I stayed focused on what God was telling me and I stayed prayed up. I even sang in the choir several Sundays. Each song I sang ministered to me because I was tired of being spiritually weak, diseased, and tired. I knew that I needed to get help with my depression sooner than later, so I started counseling sessions with Dr. Biana Daper. She gave me some assignments to complete about my life and things I wanted to accomplish. She helped me to realize my worth and how no one can take it away from me. I shared with her how I've always wanted to start a business to empower young girls and work with girls in the foster care system. This was always a passion of mine and something that I've always wanted to do. She asked me to write out a plan and make it happen. I completed my sessions with Dr. Daper and she complimented me on my growth from when she first met me. I started to write a business plan and got started on my new endeavors.

Let's get back to Myra. One day the staff received an email that Myra was leaving. Just about the entire staff was overfilled with joy. Some were dancing in the aisles and some were praising God. I just sat at my desk and praised Him silently. I knew that God was moving, and it was all a part of the process. I knew that my destiny was tied to the small things that God was asking me to do and He was only asking me to pass the test. I believed that God handpicked me to complete a task. God kept reminding me of Romans 8:18 *For I reckon that the sufferings of this present time are not worthy to be compared with the glory which shall be revealed in us.*

FROM SHACKLES TO PRAISES

Later Myra met with the staff to announce she was leaving, and she started to cry. I did not feel sorry for Myra, but I never wished anything bad on her. At that moment, God was telling me that she was a defeated enemy. Bondage was finally being broken and I started to see it all around me. I just thought to myself that the devil's time was up. My focus wasn't on Myra but on the plans that God had for my life. I finally realized that God used Myra to feed my nest. She hated me, but God used her as part of His plan.

After Myra left I was for sure I would be placed back in my position and things would change. Once again God told me to hush my mouth and let Him rule over all things. He told me to do what I needed to do, and He would handle the rest. So, I did exactly what He told me to do. I took my hands off the situation and I continued obeying Him every day. I may slip up from time to time and pick it back up, but I always find a way to steer myself back to what He has for me. Sometimes I ask myself why I allowed myself to get so depressed and why did I let the devil take over my life. God reminded me that I'm human and asked me to find my wings to do things I don't think I can do.

I'm still working at Society, still sitting in the corner that Myra put me in minding my business, and still trusting and believing that God has a bigger and better plan for me. I continue to ask God to protect me from my enemies and He revealed to me Psalms 27:5- *For in the time of trouble He shall hide me in His pavilion; in the secret of His tabernacle shall He hide me; He shall set me upon a rock.*

I understand that God was hiding me until He said it is time to be revealed. He does it every time. God still hasn't revealed why I had to go through this, but I don't mind waiting on Him. He's just told me that it'll all be worth it in the end. As for Myra using God's name in vain, that's between her and God. Exodus 20:7 states *You shall not misuse the name of the Lord your God, for the Lord will not hold anyone guiltless who misuses His name.* Hebrews 10:30 states, *For we know Him that hath said, 'Vengeance belongeth unto Me, I will recompense,' saith the Lord. And again, The Lord shall judge His people.* Therefore, it was not my place to judge what Myra had done to me. I finally stopped listening to my flesh and continued climbing the wall of greatness.

God reminded me that I could not control someone's negative behavior, but I could control how long I participated in it. I may never know why God placed Myra in my path, but I know it's not a coincidence. I don't know if God placed her in my path to push me to live out my dreams or if Satan assigned demons to stop God's answer from coming to me. I believed that I was a good leader when I was working in my position with Society, but God was calling me to lead in a different way. I've learned that He strategically lines up every person, every detail, and every step of your life. He was only waiting on me to do my part and not miss the opportunity to do well. He knew every battle I would face and every dream I would accomplish. He was only getting me prepared for my destiny. The forces that were for me were greater than the forces that were against me. He put the dreams in my heart and I plan to fulfill them. This attack drew greatness out of me

FROM SHACKLES TO PRAISES

that I didn't know I had. I kept wondering why God was giving me this assignment and he said because I thought I was too small. He told me that I was much bigger than who I thought I was.

You may be wondering why I didn't find another job. I applied to numerous positions and received notices that I was highly qualified and referred but not selected. When I got the first couple of notices, I got discouraged. God kept reminding me that He had a different plan for my life and career. After a while I would get the notices, read them, and learned to smile and say next. He reminded me that what's in my future is greater than what is in my past. I thought I was weak, but God had to show me just how strong I was. Believe and trust the process.

My message to anyone reading this is to continue walking by faith and not by sight. God hears your every prayer and sees your every cry. Don't try to fight things alone. Always go to Him and He will lead and guide you. Remember the reason why some people have turned against you and walked away from you without reason has nothing to do with you. It is because He has removed them from your life because they cannot go where God is taking you. They would only hinder you at the next level because they have already served their purpose in your life. Let them go and keep it moving. Continue to ignore the enemies and you will get to the place where the serpents cannot get to you anymore. You must believe that greater is coming your way. I don't know what tomorrow holds for me, but I know who holds tomorrow. My mind was so preoccupied with other things that it was hard for me to hear God, so He had to catch my attention during my sleep through dreams. If God can do it for me, He can bring you out of any situation you may be going through. I know that He is not finished with me yet and there's much more coming my way. I thought that life was the way it was supposed to be but now I know that God wanted more. As Pastor Marvin said one Sunday when God is ready He will show up and shut down the whole show. This was such a powerful Word to me. I will continue to obey God's Word and let Him take the wheel. Hopefully, I will have a Part 2 to my story so that I can share with you how Jesus showed up and shut down the show. You can make it!

About Cassandra Fooks

My name is Cassandra Fooks, and I am the Founder of Glory Girls Company which is a 501(c)(3) non-profit organization focused on empowerment, self-awareness, and promoting community outreach activities. Glory Girls focuses on empowering girls to overcome the challenges of negative influences and create a positive change within themselves as well as their communities. I'm passionate about empowering future leaders and I remain confident that I can help my community grow and thrive, one leader at a time. I believe that attacks draw greatness and I'm here to help our girls be great and successful. Glory Girls is my way of making positive change in the community. I wish to engage with other non-profits and leaders throughout the world to reach our young future leaders.

Contact

Email - clfooks@yahoo.com
Facebook - Cassandra Fooks and/or Glory Girls
Instagram - Glory Girls Co
Website – glorygirls.org

Cassandra's Acknowledgements

First and foremost, I'd like to thank my Lord and Savior, Jesus Christ, for keeping me during a dark time. I've learned that trials come as a test of our faith, and I thank You God for seeing me through. Special thanks to Ms. LaKesha L. Williams, the founder of Vision to Fruition for allowing God to use her talents and expertise in putting together this special project.

My amazing and devoted husband deserves many accolades. He was always by my side and reminded me I am highly favored by God. Because of his constant words of encouragement and inspiration, I stepped out on faith and shared my testimony. Thank you, hubby, for your support.

My family has been an amazing support system for me during this time. I want to thank my two wonderful children for believing that their mom is a hero. I would like to thank my mother who prayed for me when I didn't even know it. I want to thank my sisters for the many phone calls, prayers, and real talk. They always reminded me no weapon formed against me shall prosper. And to my late father and mother-in-law, although you're not here, I can still hear you encouraging me from heaven. I want to thank my Pastor for his leadership and sacrificing his time to bring others closer to God. He never knew any details of what I was going through, but the Holy Spirit allowed him to teach and preach the right message at the right time. I thank the many friends (you know who you are) for keeping me encouraged and lifted up. You were always an excellent source of inspiration.

FROM SHAME TO SHALOM

Shame: a painful feeling or humiliation or distress caused by the consciousness of wrong or foolish behavior

Shalom: peace

"For I am confident of this very thing, that He who has begun a good work in you will perfect it until the day of Christ Jesus." Philippians 1:6

In the eighth grade, I read a book called The Scarlet Letter. In short, the book is about a married woman who has an affair that produces a child as a result. In the town where she lives, she is publicly shamed for her indiscretions and is forced to wear a scarlet, gold-embroidered patch of cloth in the shape of an "A."

If you are like me, this story sounds familiar to you. It sounds familiar because many of us carry shame around in our hearts and minds in the same way the character in this story did on

FROM SHAME TO SHALOM

her chest. There are things we have said and things we have done that we carry around like a bright red ketchup stain on a crisp white shirt. It wasn't until I was having a conversation with one of my dear covenant sisters that I realized I was still carrying the sin stain from things I did in my adolescence and young adulthood.

Between the ages of five and nine years of age, I was raped and molested by five different individuals, four males and one female. I was so young I didn't really understand what was happening or going on, but these series of unfortunate events set in motion God's plan and purpose for my life. Statistics show that one of two things happen for women who have experienced sexual trauma, they either become very, very, promiscuous or they land on the other end of the spectrum with no desire for sex or intimacy.

For years I believed I was on the other end of the spectrum with no desire for sex or intimacy, but I kept finding myself in these situationships with men, where I'd draw a line which stopped just short of sexual intercourse. Psychologically I felt like I was damaged goods, so any attention I could get from a male was good enough for me, even if it was just temporary as a means for him to attempt to "get some." Emotionally I was confused. I knew what I was doing was wrong but as long as I wasn't having sex I was justified in my acts, because premarital sex was a sin. Spiritually I was dead. I knew of God and had seen Him work in various ways throughout my life, but I did not know Him or have an active intimate relationship with Him. I'd, in a sense, turned my back on Him because I was trying to fill a void only He could fill. Physically I was not engaged or aroused and often wondered why I kept allowing myself to be in these situations in the first place just to try to get a boyfriend or please a man.

So, I wasn't promiscuous in the sense of having multiple sexual partners, but I was promiscuous in the sense allowing myself to be prematurely exposed to things I had no business being engaged in. I exposed myself to sinful acts which opened doors in my heart and mind that should have never been opened. I exposed myself to men who had not paid the price of admission called marriage.

As a result of my actions, even after I came to know Christ and began a personal relationship with Him, shame followed me around like a nagging little sister or little brother but I never acknowledged it or even knew it was there, instead in manifested in a variety of different ways, like in my confidence, my self-esteem, my body image and the value that I placed on myself.

I knew the sins I'd committed were wrong, but I also knew my sins were covered by the Blood of Christ, but the disconnect came in me not actively believing and applying what I knew. Not only that, secrecy prohibited me from really addressing firstly the rape and molestation, and secondly the after effects of experiencing sexual trauma. For years I kept the rape and molestation a secret. It happened when I was five, it was exposed when I was 21 and I didn't seek the help of a professional Christian counselor until I was 29. That's a total of

FROM SHAME TO SHALOM

24 years I was held captive to a skewed view of sex, men and myself. That's more than 15 years of walking around wearing a scarlet letter "A" that only I could see but I felt like everyone could see and knew my indiscretions. That's more than 15 years of shame, that needed to be addressed and dealt with, so I could arrive at this place to be able to share my story with you and help you begin washing the stain of shame from your heart, mind, and soul.

Here is the blessing of it all. God washed the stain of my sin and removed my scarlet letter in less than 24 hours. How? I exposed the secret, recognized the shame and how it was manifesting in my life, and resolved within myself to share my story. No, I am not saying it will happen this fast for everyone, but the point I want to drive home is that God is faithful to complete the good work He began in us before the foundation of the earth.

While the earth was still formless and empty, and darkness was over the surface of the deep, and the Spirit of God was hovering over the waters, you were but a thought in God's mind. Jeremiah 1:5 says, "Before I formed you in the womb I knew you, and before you were born I consecrated you; I have appointed you a prophet to the nations." Psalm 139:16 says, "You saw me before I was born. Every day of my life was recorded in your book. Every moment was laid out before a single day had passed."

You see, God knew us, He already knew, the mistakes you would make, He already knew the sins you'd commit, He already knew the foolish behavior you'd engage in and He already made room in the plan of your life to cover those sins and mistakes. God's grace covers a multitude of sins. It is not God's desire for us to live in sorrow and shame. It is His desire that we live in peace and harmony with Him. It is His desire that we commune in intimate covenant and relationship with Him. But it is impossible for us to do that if we are living in shame, tormented by the thoughts we allow the enemy to place in our minds about our past.

God has many names but the one that applied here is Jehovah Shalom. Jehovah means Lord, Holiness, Truth revealer, righteousness and redemption. The word shalom is a harmony or reconciliation of relationship based upon the completion of a transaction, the payment of a debt, the giving of satisfaction.

God wants to expose the shame we carry (Truth Revealer), put us in right standing with Him (righteousness) and redeem us from our wrong, sinful, foolish behaviors (redemption). God sent His Son Jesus as the payment of the debt we created through sin (shalom). God used Jesus to reconcile us back to Himself.

God revealed five truths about His peace:

1. Jesus provided our peace for us by His own death.

Romans 5:1 says, "Therefore being justified by faith, we have peace with God through our Lord Jesus Christ." We now have

FROM SHAME TO SHALOM

peace with God, which may differ from peaceful feelings such as tranquility and calmness. Peace with God means that we have been reconciled with Him. There is no more hostility because of us, and no shame or sin is blocking our relationship with Him. Peace with God is possible only because Jesus paid the price for our sins through His death on the Cross.

Romans 5:9-10 says, "For if, when we were enemies, we were reconciled to God by the death of his Son, much more, being reconciled, we shall be saved by his life." The love that caused Christ to die is the same love that sends the Holy Spirit to love in us and guide us every day. The power that raised Christ from the dead is the same power that saved you and is available to you in your daily life. It's this same power that trumps shame if you allow it to. Be assured that, having begun a life with Christ, you have a reserve of power and love to call on each day, for help to meet every challenge or trial. You can pray for God's power and love as you need it.

2. The measure of peace that we have in Him is determined by our sanctification and trust in Him.

Philippians 4:6-7 says, "Be careful for nothing; but in everything by prayer and supplication with thanksgiving let your requests be made known unto God. And the peace of God, which passeth all understanding, shall keep your hearts and minds through Christ Jesus." I was not satisfied with myself because of the shame which trickled down into me not being satisfied with God or even trusting Him. I was anxious all the time but imagine being anxious for nothing! It seems like an impossibility. We all have worries on the job, in our homes, at school, but Paul's advice is to turn your worries into prayers. Do you want to worry less? Then pray more! Whenever you start to worry, stop and pray.

3. God's peace is different from the world's peace.

John 14: 27 says, "Peace I leave you; My peace I give to you; not as the world gives do I give to you. Do not let your heart be troubled, nor let it be fearful." The end result of the Holy Spirit's work in our lives is deep and lasting peace. Unlike worldly peace, which is usually defined as the absence of conflict, this peace is confident assurance in any circumstance and with Christ's peace, we have no need to fear the past, present or future. If your life is full of shame, allow the Holy Spirit to fill you with Christ's peace.

True peace is not found in positive thinking, in absence of conflict or in good feelings. It comes from knowing that God is in control. It comes from knowing that God already knew where you'd be right now. It comes from knowing nothing is a secret from Him and He loves you unconditionally anyway. He knows the dirty little nasty things you have done and what you thought were secret. God is El Roi, which means the God who sees. He knew it, He saw it, and He still loves every ounce of you, unconditionally. Our citizenship in Christ's kingdom is sure, our destiny is set, and we can have victory over shame. Let God's peace guard your heart against shame.

4. The peace of God comes through spiritual-mindedness.

FROM SHAME TO SHALOM

Romans 8:6 says, "For to be carnally minded is death; but to be spiritually minded is life and peace." Paul divides people into two categories – those who let themselves be controlled by their sinful natures, and those who follow after the Holy Spirit. All of us would be in the first category if Jesus hadn't offered us a way out. Once we have said yes to Jesus, we will want to continue following Him, because His way brings life and peace. Daily we must consciously choose to center our lives on God. Use the Bible to discover God's guidelines, and then follow them. In every perplexing situation, ask yourself, "What would Jesus want me to do?" When the Holy Spirit points out what is right, do it eagerly. When the Holy Spirit points out shame and sin, like He did for me, begin taking steps to address it immediately.

5. Peace is part of the fruit of the Holy Spirit.

Galatians 5:22 says, "But the fruit of the Spirit is love, joy, peace, longsuffering, gentleness, goodness, faithfulness, gentleness, self-control; against such there is no law." The fruit of the Spirit is the spontaneous work of the Holy Spirit in us. The Spirit produces these character traits that are found in the nature of Christ. They are by-products of Christ's control – we can't obtain them by trying to get them without His help. If we want the fruit of the Spirit to grow in us, we must join our lives to His. We must know Him, love Him, remember Him and imitate Him. As a result, we will fulfill the intended purpose of the law, to love God and our neighbors and we will live a life of peace, shame-free.

In conclusion, there is no peace besides that which can come by way of Christ. There is no other way.

Know Jesus - Know Peace -- No Jesus - No Peace

When we have a relationship with God through His Son, Jesus; He becomes our Jehovah-Shalom - the One who brings the peace that passes all understanding and trumps all shame.

About LaKesha L. Williams

LaKesha L. Williams, acclaimed author, speaker and minister of the Gospel of Jesus Christ, was born to parents Doris & Cleo Williams in Raleigh, North Carolina in 1983. To know LaKesha is to experience a calming spirit infused with gut-wrenching laughter at unexpected times. She has a passion for giving, which is demonstrated wholeheartedly through her founding of Born Overcomers Inc. a nonprofit organization & movement dedicated to promoting the belief that we were all Born to Overcome.

LaKesha is the Lead Visionary behind Overcomers HQ, which is dedicated to helping others overcome, thrive & bring their visions to fruition. Overcomers HQ is comprised of Born Overcomers Inc., Vision to Fruition LLC, LaKesha L. Williams Ministries, Team Overcomers & Overcomers Bling.

She has authored eight books, including two bestsellers; and is also a featured co-author in Open Your G.I.F.T.S. presented by actress & comedian Kim Coles. She is also the Owner of Vision to Fruition, a consulting firm dedicated to helping others bring their personal, business, ministry & nonprofit visions to fruition.

In 2015, LaKesha received the Sistas Inspiring Sistas Phenomenal Woman Award, and since has gone on to become the 2016 Indie Author Legacy Award Recipient in the Author on the Rise category; a 2016 Metro Phenomenal Woman Honoree; a 2017 TDK Publishing Author of the Year nominee & the 2018 iShine Awards winner for Author of the

Year.

LaKesha, as a virgin herself, is also an advocate of abstinence, purity & virginity until marriage. Currently, LaKesha resides in Southern Maryland & enjoys serving in the community, fellowshipping with her church family at The Remnant of Hope International Church in Prince Frederick Maryland under the leadership of Pastor Margo Gross and spending time with her family & friends watching movies, sharing stories & creating new memories.

Contact

Websites: overcomershq.com and vision-fruition.com
Phone #: 240-343-3563
Facebook: www.facebook.com/lakesha.williams
Facebook Pages: Born Overcomers Inc. and Vision to Fruition
Twitter & IG: @overcomershq and @vision-fruition

LaKesha's Acknowledgments

First and foremost, I want to thank my Lord and Savior Jesus Christ for becoming the Ultimate Sacrifice for my sin and for being the Ultimate Example of how I should live my life. Lord Jesus, everything I am, everything I have and everything I could ever hope to be is You. Thank You for saving me and loving me unconditionally. I love You forever!

To my Parents - Cleo R. Williams Jr. and Doris M. Williams - Mom, thank you for raising, nurturing, loving and supporting me unconditionally in everything! Dad, thank you for always being my biggest fan, you are my real-life Superhero. I love you both! God knew when He entrusted me to you that you both had everything I needed to be the Woman of God I am today!

To my Siblings – Rachel - thank you for always challenging and pushing me to go higher, do better and be more.

Travis, thank you for always being concerned in the way that only big brothers can. I love you both.

To my Inner Circle – Dana McCollum, my oldest and dearest friend, thank you for your continual and unconditional love and support. We have truly weathered the storms of life and friendship together over the years. I love you like a fat kid loves cake and licking the plate.

Nikea Marie, my Honey Bunches, you helped restore my skewed perception of friendship and you have truly been a sister and a friend, and I cherish our relationship, always have, always will! You know I love you boo!

Chris Allen, my little Big sis, thank you for teaching me what covenant looks like and how to war on your sister's behalf. I love and appreciate you more than you'll ever know.

Latricia C. Bailey, you are an answered prayer. You are my Jonathan, my safe place, my vault, my sister, my friend, a breath of fresh air and you embody what true, unconditional, nonjudgmental friendship looks like and so much more. We are knit together and my love for you is unquestionable.

To my Covenant Circle - Thank you for praying for me, for co-laboring with me and for locking arms with me in Covenant and Christian Unity as we press toward the mark for the prize of the high calling of God in Christ Jesus! Friendships come to an end, but a covenant is forever! I love you all!

To my Born Overcomers Team and Supporters - Thank you for executing every task I've asked of you and thank you for your continuous prayers, support, and love! Also, thank you to any and everyone who has ever supported me and the ministry in any way, I appreciate you!

To my Vision to Fruition Team – Thank you for your tireless work to help bring visions to fruition on a daily basis! There would be no Vision to Fruition without you! I appreciate you immensely!

GOOD GRIEF: IN MY FATHER'S EYES

I'm done. Dead done. Sick and tired of being sick and tired. Simply done. Done with what, you ask? Done with DEATH and GRIEF.

It has been said that worry refuses to share the heart with gratitude. This is so true. Yet when it comes to grieving and death, they haven't learned this valuable lesson of the heart. Instead, they continue to take up residence in a place of the heart like uninvited and unwelcome visitors. Death is inevitable, and we are not meant to live on Earth forever. Those of us who believe in Jesus as our Lord and Savior have Heaven to look forward to after death, but those who don't believe, will suffer an eternity in Hell. The thought of this is too horrible for words! I wouldn't wish Hell on anyone, however, death in general is still a hard thing to process even for the hopeful.

Grief can be the result of a death or loss of many things:

GOOD GRIEF

Family. Friends. Relationships. Children. Health. Pet. Pregnancy. Job. Finances. House. A Lifestyle and even a dream. The list goes on depending on your view of the value of that loss. I have experienced losing all of these at various times in my life.

Lost my grandmother. She was the only grandparent I ever knew. She was witty, fun, and had a zeal for life – I loved. She told great stories, made good food, and was comical to be around. I Lost a cousin who dropped dead unexpectedly. She left an 8-month-old behind. I had given birth three months earlier to my oldest son, Tyler. Her loss made me cherish motherhood even more than I did. I lost my nephew, Jeffrey, to Meningitis while he was finishing up college. He was more like a son to me, and we were very close. He was found dead in his apartment in Chester, Pennsylvania, with a hospital wristband still on him because he had just been released from the emergency room. Broke my heart.

I was sick the night before I found out he died. I was in so much pain my husband, Michael, called my doctor. At some point in middle of the night I had a "vision" of a tall lamp being knocked over, and a long drawer being pulled open. I awoke when heard a voice call my name. This has happened before, and I always say, "Speak Lord." The Lord responded this time saying that He would reveal it later. I went back to sleep. When I woke up later that morning, my mom called to tell me the terrible news. I was devastated.

She, my father, and I went to Pennsylvania to identify Jeffrey's body, but stopped at his apartment beforehand. There was a tall lamp knocked over. Later, at the hospital, would be my first time at a morgue. This was the vision of a long drawer pulled open that God had showed me. I touched Jeffrey's forehead. It was cold and hollow like a shell. He wasn't there. I couldn't feel his spirit anymore. I understood now how people really are created as spiritual beings in earthly bodies.

In 2009, I lost a lot. Lost a baby when I miscarried. I had recently found out that I was pregnant, now my baby was gone. I briefly lost my health to Swine Flu and bronchitis for a week. We lost our dog, D.J. when he ran away. He was found a couple weeks later with a cross on a chain around his neck. Lost my father to Pulmonary Fibrosis on the Monday before Thanksgiving Day. Five days later, Michael, who had been on dialysis for over a year, received a pancreas and kidney transplant. I was grieving and grateful all at the same time. I was angry at God for taking my father, but grateful that my husband was getting new organs. A few months later, we almost lost our house to foreclosure. We even lost our electricity when we couldn't afford the bill. Eventually we moved out.

In the past few years I lost my best friend, Priscilla, and a close friend, Ivana, and others to Cancer. Priscilla died on the 4th of July 2015. That was a true Independence Day for her after suffering from Leukemia for a few years. I helped coordinate the transport of her body from hospice to the crematory, and then assisted in putting her in a body bag. Then, exhausted and overwhelmed from the ordeal, I broke down in tears!

GOOD GRIEF

Ivana died nine months later at home while I was by her side. She had a glimpse of Heaven, and longed to go.

More deaths came from family and friends, and several mothers of church members. A couple years ago, I lost three cousins from the same family just a few months apart (daughter, mother, and son) and several other loved ones that year. I found myself in a place of grieving for people that were hurting everywhere. I didn't know how to unload this bag of sorrow. Though I know joy should have been there, it didn't feel like it. We, who are saved, have hope in Christ as the Word of God says. It is true. Yet the pain from mourning doesn't always seem to agree.

I was talking one day with Tyler about his friends saying how glad I am that he has good friends to talk with. It made me tear up as I thought about how a few of my closest friends and family were now gone! While I know I have hope in Christ, somehow, I still hurt from not having them here to share my journey and successes with me. This time in my life is so pivotal, and I am so blessed to have been a part of such good friendships and relationships all around. I am reminded that while, YES, I am missing my loved ones who have departed this world, I am reassured of the love of Christ and the favor of God's grace. He walks with me daily to provide the comfort of hope that one day I will truly grieve no more.

I still remember the day that I last saw my earthly father. I looked into his eyes and suddenly the years of worry, pain, and sorrow were no longer there. It was as if he knew his time on earth was drawing near. His comforting smile, and quiet, calm way of expressing himself came through his face with just one look. This great man of God and Marine that had protected me as a child and raised me with all the provisions a daughter would ever need, was now facing his meet with his Maker. Thank you, Heavenly Father, for blessing me with an earthly father like no other. He taught me how to be a lady. He showed me how to have grace, dignity, and class. I am the woman of God he desired me to be because of the great love and favor God gave me through an earthly father like my daddy. I am grateful that He didn't leave me fatherless when He called him to come home to Heaven. I dedicate this writing to God first, my Heavenly Father, and to David Lewis Cox, Sr., my earthly father, for allowing healing to take place as he left earth.

We have celebrated many Thanksgiving Days since my dad passed away, but 2017 was the first time my mother mentioned that she didn't know if she wanted to celebrate with her family because Thanksgiving "is on the same day that David died." I really think she was feeling his loss more than in the past because she hadn't been feeling well. I had come to terms with the fact that I would miss him every holiday. No one could tell jokes and stories like he could. Our family gatherings were always fun! That year we ended up going to my cousin's house and had a good time. I still miss my papa so much. We talked almost daily. He always encouraged me to lean on the Lord and stay close to His Word. He also knew how it felt to lose his life and live to tell about it.

GOOD GRIEF

He had been hospitalized, with a breathing tube. He stopped breathing.

Flatlined.

He described this time as his Heaven experience. He said he saw Himself hovering over bones of dead bodies, then a great light appeared that was too awesome for words. He felt an indescribable peace. He didn't want to leave. He was on his way to eternal rest with his Lord.

Resuscitation interrupts!

Papa is back! God wasn't ready for him to come home just yet. Dad had to live to tell others about this phenomenal experience! And he did! I am grateful for the death, burial, and resurrection of my first father, my Lord and Savior Jesus the Christ. Because of Him, I was able to celebrate many holidays with my earthly father, who set the example of the kind of love and care of what my Heavenly father wants for me. Thank you, Lord, for reminding me of this.

Paul says in Philippians 3, we should choose to *"count everything as loss because of the surpassing worth of knowing Christ Jesus"* and *"press on toward the goal for the prize of the upward call of God in Christ Jesus."* God showed me that like Christ, I have chosen to leave worldly things behind to press for His amazing love and life!

Like Christ, I am experiencing a "resurrection" and coming out of "dead" things. Resurrection is the concept of coming back to life after death. In several ancient religions, a dying-and-rising god is a deity which dies and resurrects. The death and resurrection of Jesus, an example of resurrection, is the central focus of Christianity. So, while I know death and grief are inevitable, God has revived me, and I am no longer smothered by either!

The week my father died, in my spirit I kept hearing the phrase, "I dreamed a dream." I didn't know what this meant until God revealed it Tuesday, December 1, 2009, at 5:40 a.m. He divinely gave me the poetic words my father would have said if he were still alive. I spoke them at his funeral.

I dreamed a dream today, and all the world was right. Just before my weary eyes was a vision of gold. Pearly gates and a golden pathway, skies of an iridescent bright blue hue.

My body didn't ache. My feet were brand new. My heart suffered no more, for all my suffering was through. I had a great peace and joy I never knew.

All my years of waiting had finally ended, and now I was going home. As I turned to my loved ones to say, "goodbye", I was ready to close my eyes and let my dream come true.

Don't be sad for me, I'm truly blessed. God brought me on home for my final rest. Think of me often as you enjoy your remaining time. Life is but a moment, and you don't have time to whine. Stop murmuring and complaining, and letting

GOOD GRIEF

anger and pain be gained.

Enjoy life on earth freely, till the day you are totally free. Forget about the past, you can't change it. Live for today. Make amends and forgive. Treat each moment like precious gold, for there is no time to waste.

Show respect, and love without fear. Be a part of the solution and not the problem. Learn to forgive and forget, but trust God through the process. He won't ever let you down. As for me, I am now totally set free. I am no longer bound. I lived a peaceful, simple life and now you must learn to go on.

I dreamed a dream today, and now my dream has come true. No more pain and suffering for me, I am totally made new. Embracing the great God, I served on earth, and living in my mansion without pain. Living in love not hate and enjoying my life forever more.

God made my dream come true today. He made me brand new. Are you ready to dream a dream like me? Then start by trusting God to lead your life. Don't settle for anything less. Don't live in sin, anger or bitterness. Perfect love casts out all fear, and your time to go may be drawing near. Don't waste it by looking back at all your mistakes. Triumph daily in every way, by looking to God to direct your path and focus on Him each day. This day would have come to pass with and without you. When will you start trusting God to see your dream come true?

LATRICIA C. BAILEY

"I cried out to the Lord, and He heard me from His Temple in Jerusalem. Then I lay down and slept in peace and woke up safely, for the Lord was watching over me."
Psalm 3:4-5 TLB

I spoke those words nine years ago but didn't really know how to process them then. It has only been after suffering so much loss that God allowed me to understand how to truly go through both death and grief with a peaceful hope only the unwavering love of God brings. Now that's GOOD GRIEF in my Father's Eyes.

About Latricia C. Bailey

Helping others discover and develop their purpose in life is one way to describe the life of Latricia C. Bailey. She is inspired by people from all walks of life. Although Latricia is a native of Washington, DC, she considers many places worldwide as part of her upbringing. From the age of six to ten years old she lived in Thailand and Mexico and traveled to China, Indonesia, Malaysia, Singapore, Japan, Paris, and other places until she and her family settled back in the Washington Metropolitan area at the age of ten.

Latricia graduated with a Bachelor of Arts degree in Journalism from Delaware State University in 1990. Her degree and training have served her well in her professional life. She is an entrepreneur with years of experience in administration, management, event planning, publishing, consulting, and sales from various companies including the National Academy of Sciences, the National Academy Press.

Latricia is a dramatist, and playwright, known for her Bag Lady Series productions that minister to women of all backgrounds. She is an active member with the Youth and Family Ministry at her home church, Sharon Bible Fellowship in Lanham, Maryland.

Her desire is to see families live the quality of life and freedom that is afforded in the body of Christ. She is a co-laborer in the Anointed Women in Christ ministry which dedicates itself to "setting the captives free" through workshops, conferences, and various forms of ministering God's word through resources and productions.

Latricia lives by the life verse, "Above all, love each other deeply, because love covers over a multitude of sins." 1 Peter 4:8.

Latricia Bailey has been married for over 20 years to her awesome husband, Michael Bailey, and has three amazing children, Tyler, Gabrielle, and Jonathan. They currently reside in Maryland.

Contact

Facebook: Latricia C Bailey
Twitter: @lb_latricia
Instagram: LatriciaLadybagBailey
Linked In: Latricia Bailey
Email: latriciabailey@outlook.com
Phone: (301)744-7021

Latricia's' Acknowledgements

I also dedicate this writing to my mother, Cora E. Cox, who showed me that before I could be a lady, I needed to realize my value and worth as a woman of God. I thank her for this. I dedicate this book to my loving and faithful husband, Michael O. Bailey, for all your support and tireless effort to help make my dreams come true. Thank you for helping me to pour out my passion. I love you always! Thank you to my strong and courageous, insightful son, Tyler David Bailey. We gave you your grandfather's name as your middle name to honor him, and you wear it proudly. Thank you my sweet, angel pie, Gabrielle J. Bailey, for your spirit of helps and compassion that shine through radiantly. Thank you, Lord, for my energetic, and gregarious son, Jonathan Thomas Bailey, who always reminds me that, *"I can do all things through Christ who makes me strong."* Philippians 4:13

God, my God, You are Alpha, Omega, the beginning and the end. Is there anything too hard for You? I know the answer is "no".

HOW HOPE HELPED HEAL

Glory to God the battle doesn't belong to me. God has brought me through so much. At age eighteen, I had my first nervous breakdown. I had no clue about depression, let alone postpartum depression. I had recently miscarried and had tons of things going wrong. I ended up hospitalized a in mental institution where I was diagnosed with depression, and severe anxiety, including PTSD. I relocated after being released.

The sunshine state seemed to bring me great joy once I moved. I started to attend my grandma's church, and even got a job in the day school. I attended a weekend retreat called Teens Encountering Christ. Nobody there knew me or knew about my past, and this was so refreshing. On the second night we could link up with the pastor and pray. He was a God-send and had answers I was seeking. He told me I was battling a demon or two in my head, but since I had

HOW HOPE HELPED HEAL

Jesus in my heart I wouldn't be possessed. Wow! He told me what to do and prayed with me. Things got better. God gave me a newfound hope in Him and reminded me I have a blessed life ahead. I got engaged and pregnant again. I had another miscarriage and suffered great depression and anxiety, so I decided to moved home. I did not realize that though I has defeated the demons, I still had a chemical imbalance. I still do, but God is healing me in time.

This was in, 2002, and my baby brother's two and a half-year-old younger brother was beaten to death by his mom's boyfriend. I had another breakdown. Not understanding everything that I was dealing with and being so soon after my miscarriage and depression, I was broken. I ended up back in the hospital, this time in the mental ward. I remember bits and pieces of this time. I would sing about Jesus' love and the Bible. In art I made an eagle as a reminder of those who wait on the Lord. I helped others and finally got off suicide watch. I had hoped this wasn't the end of my good days, but another new beginning.

Since that time, I gave birth to my daughter who's now thirteen years old. She is a miracle baby. She was my fourth pregnancy and a high risk that doctors thought might be born sick. God however showed Himself faithful again. He blessed us with hope. We had struggled on and off with my mental illness, but God has always provided and protected us.

I had been questioned about my faith, my love for God, and others, even for self. However, God continued to bring me through. He has given me hope, and now some understanding. I was in the car driving, praying, crying out for relief for answers. I said, "I am tired God. "Why does the bottom always fall out? Will I ever be stable?" And God spoke to me. He asked why I was ashamed for what He brought me out of. He had healed me, protected me, and still continues to be faithful. Why do I feel ashamed or embarrassed because I have a simple chemical imbalance that can be helped with medication? If I had a cold, I would take medication, but because some people claim me to be fighting demons, etc., I almost let myself forget who and what God said I am. He never counted me out because this was going to be used for my good and His glory. One thing is for sure my hope in God and His word and relationship with me, helps me overcome.

When I look back at how faithful God has been and all the things He is doing now. I have so much hope and trust that mental illness isn't my identity. It is a chemical imbalance that is helped by using medicine to produce the chemicals needed for balance. However, no medicine can fix a broken mind. A relationship with God and His healing, convictions, and promises to give a good life gives hope and healing. My thoughts need to change. I need to speak positive and real things to myself and others. The medicine can help treat but hope in God will help heal.

Since high school I have been struggling trying to find out where I went wrong. How did this happen to me? Broken yet blessed. I love God, but, where is He? Why am I not enough?

HOW HOPE HELPED HEAL

Will I ever get better? I'm tired of being sick and tired. Stop accusing me of being lazy. Don't let me use this as an excuse to stay stuck. I must keep hope in the Lord for He has helped me overcome everything until this point. He will continue to bring me through. Notice how we have to change our thoughts and focus. I have to accept that I have a health problem. However, I don't have to let it define or dictate me. There are reasons I can't do things sometimes and other times there are excuses. However, I'd rather trust in God and all the goodness He has for me. First, I must admit, gain knowledge, and take steps to keep moving forward. Two hospitalizations, tons of doctor's appointments, medicines, tests, therapy, opinions, prayers, and God's faithfulness, love, mercy, and grace I am still overcoming. I learned that the same treatment does not work for everyone. Not everyone has the support system I have. However, everyone can find hope in Jesus. There is healing, deliverance and love in Him.

I don't look like what I have been through. Right now, I'm doing my first book collaboration. I am working on a multinational corporation business deal. I am working on my own business plan. Looking at me you wouldn't necessarily know my diagnosis which has changed several times by different doctors. However, I still stick to mental illness to cover all of them. I am blessed, I have a good life, and an amazing life bigger than me ahead. My hope is in God and His words. My hope has been my strength at times and taken off the limits and judgments I and others have placed on me. God however has set me free, and although I still struggle with depression and anxiety I'm learning to change my mindset.

SHANA QUIRK

My hope grows as God continues to deliver me, and only He sets me free from strongholds.

About Shana Quirk

Hi, my name is Shana Quirk. I'm a 35-year-old mom of one. I was born in Northern Indiana. I graduated high school in 2001. I'm returning to college for an elementary education degree. I enjoy life most days, however I am grateful every day. I have two brothers and a sister and currently two nephews and nieces. I am a woman of many hats. Yet I find myself daydreaming and brainstorming about the goals I will like to accomplish. I have many years of experience in early childhood education. I would like to start a private preschool, a training and education program for early childhood education, and become a legal private consultant for early childhood education. I must admit hope has got me through tough times and helped me hold on to a blessed life. I suffer from mental illness. I was first diagnosed after graduating high school in 2001.

Contact

Email: shanaquirk@gmail.com
Facebook: Shana ISWI Quirk & Shana Gracious Quirk

Shana's Acknowledgments

I want to thank God for this opportunity and for bringing me through as an overcomer. I want to thank my family and my mom, Sharon, for supporting me and believing in this and blessing me with the finances to participate. I want to thank each and every one of my family and friends that's been there and showed me love and all the people that God has used in my life and all the people that He's going to continue to use to help me go forward in life. I thank my daughter, Alyson. She is a motivation to keep striving to do better. God uses her in a mighty way to teach me. I want to thank LaKesha and everyone who joined to make this a success. I want to thank my best friend, Tonya, for allowing me to not just brush it off but to actually consider and pray about doing this project. I want to thank all the overcomers that will be reading this book. God bless.

IMAGINE ME

Confused, yet convinced that I must have heard God wrong, I closed my journal, leaned back in my chair and just sat there motionless.

God, there's no way that you just whispered to me to deal with my unforgiveness.

What unforgiveness?

Yea, I know there's some things that I need to work on, but one thing's for sure un-forgiveness isn't one of them.

You see early on as a new Christian, I learned that if I wanted God to forgive me of my sins, then I had to forgive those who sinned against me. So, whenever I was offended I would quickly extend the principles of forgiveness to the offender to maintain my good standing with God. I took this principle so serious that I even forgave my abusive ex-husband and became friends with him on Facebook. Now you know that's

IMAGINE ME

forgiveness displayed to the 10th power.

More than anything, I wanted everyone that was connected to me to be able to walk in God's complete forgiveness too. Therefore, I would encourage them to follow my lead and forgive their offenders quickly and at all cost.

I sat there quietly questioning what I thought I had heard God tell me earlier, but at this point I was simply clueless.

Then as clear as day, I heard the Lord tell me, "Write down everything that ever offended you." In full confidence that there wasn't any unforgiveness resting in my heart, I quickly grabbed my pen and started writing out of obedience:

…my childhood

…family/parents

…bad relationships

…and of course,…the abuse

Then I sat back again, took a deep breath, put my pen down, looked over my paper and waited.

"You just grouped things together like a bunch of trees in a forest, but I want to deal with every branch", the Lord said.

"Huh???

What are you talking about God"?

"Write down the details of the offenses against you" said the Lord.

I picked up the pen and started writing again, but this time instead of writing down "my childhood" I wrote:

…being told that I was too dumb to make honor roll

… teased about being in Special Ed classes

… acting out and running away from home

… being bullied daily then becoming a bully to stop the abuse

…being arrested and charged with assault and battery in the 7th grade

…using drugs and alcohol to numb the pain

…failed suicide attempt

As my eyes filled with tears I whispered, "God what's going on," but He stayed silent. God, you know I've already forgiven everyone, and our relationships are good, so why do You want me to do this again" I asked, but I heard nothing. God, I don't understand"? He still said absolutely nothing.

IMAGINE ME

So instead of writing "family" I wrote;

...feeling unloved and unwanted

...not ever measuring up or being good enough

...rejection and abandonment issues resulting in low-self esteem

...years of suffering from depression

... feelings of being invisible and out of sight

...the shame of being sexually molested as a child by two family members multiple times

...miscarriage

As God continued to bring things back to my remembrance and my heart began to hurt so bad that I could hardly breathe, yet instead of writing "Bad relationships and abuse" I pressed to write;

... The doctor who convinced me to have an abortion and then killed my child.

... church hurt, abandonment and rejection from multiple places and people

DANA MCCOLLUM

...being sexually assaulted in Korea by three different men from three different organizations who were all in church leadership positions.

...being five months pregnant and then abandoned by my son's biological father at only 19 years old

... two failed marriages before I was 25 years old

...my first husband who adopted my son only to abandon him once the adoption was completed, which prevented him from receiving survival benefits from his biological father when he died.

...how he dumped me for another woman on our my 2nd Anniversary weekend

... the affair that my second husband had while I was pregnant with his child and raising his other two sons.

... being left on the side of the road on Interstate 95 at 2:30 a.m. in January with no coat or money. How I had to hitchhike with a random truck driver to a rest stop and use his quarter to call for help.

... For the physical, emotional and financial abuse that I suffered at his hands, as he beat me over and over again

... The Army police officers who ignored my cries and failed to protect me from his abuse on several occasions.

IMAGINE ME

'GOD WHAT IS GOING ON I SCREAMED?"

God said nothing!

And for over three long hours I cried... I screamed... I shouted... and yelled at the top of my voice at God! The whole time it felt as if an eruption was bubbling up at my core, and I had absolutely no control over it, so I cried out to God again in desperation

BUT I STILL HEARD NOTHING!

You see, I had no idea that I was even in bondage to unforgiveness. The root was so deeply suppressed and buried inside of me that I had even hidden it from myself. I was terrified about what God was revealing to me, but deep down inside I knew that He was exposing the enemy's tactics that were used against me and this was not going to be pretty.

I hadn't even noticed that my CD player was set on repeat and was playing the song "Imagine Me" by Kirk Franklin, softly in the background over and over. Emotionally exhausted, I just sat there and started to meditate on the words of the song while the tears slowly continued to fall down my face. The more I listened to the song the more it seemed that the words were starting to get louder and at some point, it seemed like the words were even screaming out at me;

DANA MCCOLLUM

"Imagine Me" Hero Album by Kirk Franklin, 2006

Imagine me
Loving what I see when the mirror looks at me 'cause I...

I imagine me
In a place of no insecurities
And I'm finally happy 'cause
I imagine me

Letting go of all of the ones who hurt me
'Cause they never did deserve me
Can you imagine me?
Saying no to thoughts that try to control me
Remembering all you told me
Lord, can you imagine me?
Over what my mama said
And healed from what my daddy did
And I wanna live and not read that page again

Imagine me, being free, trusting you totally, finally I can
Imagine me
I admit it was hard to see
You being in love with someone like me
But finally, I can
Imagine me

Being strong
And not letting people break me down
You won't get that joy this time around

IMAGINE ME

Can you imagine me?

Without a doubt I knew that God was speaking to me directly through this song even though it seemed as if He hadn't answered any of my questions this entire time. As I continued to recite the words of the song I could feel a gentle shift taking place in my spirit. I knew that God was doing something new. Everything that I had done prior to this day was just forgiveness surface work, but now He was pulling up unforgiveness at its roots.

God showed me that when I grouped the offenses together in categories like a bunch of trees in a forest that it distorted my vision. I was being hindered from seeing the depth of the offense and the real damage that was done on the inside of me.

You see, when you look at a forest full of trees you cannot see the true state of the tree's individual structures, branches or leaves. But if you go deeper into the forest and stand at the trunk of any individual tree, then will you be able to see the details of that particular tree and also anything that may be unhealthy or wrong with it too. God had me to write out the offenses individually, so He could show me how deeply the roots of my unforgiveness had taken up residence in my heart.

Unforgiveness is a thief. It comes to kill, steal, and destroy whomever will embrace and drink from its poison. It comes to rob you of your joy, your peace of mind, your relationships and your energy. It comes to rob you of your precious time that can never be regained or replaced. Unforgiveness is destructive, draining and very costly. It takes a lot of work to nurse this negative emotion, and oftentimes we unconsciously commit to holding on to our un-forgiveness for dear life.

You see, while we are putting all of our energy into holding onto the offense, the other person may have simply moved on and let it go. They may have even forgotten what had happened and may not be affected or phased by it anymore at all. They may have some type of addiction or mental illness that may prevent them from being remorseful or even present to the pain that they have caused you. Some people's hearts unfortunately are just so cold and selfish that they don't care if they have hurt anyone or not. In other words, our offenders may just be clueless to the mental and emotional whirlwind that their actions may have caused us.

I believe the reason that forgiveness is so hard sometimes to extend to those who hurt us, is because we feel like after what they have done to us that they simply don't deserve it. After-all, we are the one who was offended, not the other way around. It's easy to get things confused and think that forgiveness is about the person who offended us. But the truth is that it's not about them at all.

Forgiveness is a precious gift from God. He freely grants and displays this gift to us over and over again. God first offered His Forgiveness to us when His only begotten Son died on the cross for our sins and all while we were yet His enemies. God

IMAGINE ME

has already even forgiven us for all of our sins from the past, present and even the sins in the future. Through His forgiveness we have access to a loving relationship with Him. Through this relationship we are commanded to offer the same selfless act of forgiveness to those who have sinned against us, so we can receive God's forgiveness. For God's love covers a multitude of sins--ours and theirs.

Before this day, I thought I had honestly been operating in this forgiveness principle wholeheartedly, especially since I currently had good relationships with the majority of those who had hurt me. Well since God had revealed His truth about this situation to me, I knew I had to make a choice that day.

I could choose to ignore the unforgiveness that God had exposed and continue to operate on the surface like I didn't know it existed, or I could embrace the hurt and offense that was revealed and allow God to heal me once and for all.

So, I chose that day to do it God's way. I chose to allow His truth and grace to permeate every corner of my being, as I surrendered my will and my way.

In an instant God's forgiveness POURED out through me to everything listed on the paper.

It POURED out over everyone who hurt me or did me wrong.

It POURED out over everyone who didn't protect me or failed

to keep me from harm's way.

It POURED out over every disappointment and disgrace that I have ever experience.

It POURED out over all the shame, condemnation and guilt that had held me hostage.

It even POURED out over the depths of my heart where offering forgiveness to myself was not possible.

I was completely overwhelmed with emotion that I had never felt before. I jumped up and started to pace around the room, as I recited the words of the song out loud until I was able to come into agreement with the words and believed that these same words applied to me.

YES.... I COULD FINALLY IMAGINE MYSELF.... BEING FREE!!

Free to take ownership of my NEW truth and walk out my NEW declarations and decree that:

No longer will I assist God in the forgiveness process and operate as if I've been promoted to Holy Ghost Junior, Judge, and Jury. But will let God vindicate me before my offender, however He chooses to do so.

No longer will I operate through a "surface level forgiveness method" and allow unforgiveness to reign in my heart in secrecy.

IMAGINE ME

No longer will I minimize the damage that the offense has caused or ignore the imprint that the offense left on my life's traumatic disc.

No longer will I let an offense linger but will strive for resolution with my offender quickly, but only if it's healthy for me to do so. And if this is not possible or beneficial for me to do, then I will seek internal resolution within myself by providing some form of self-care to myself until my change comes.

No longer will I believe the lie that I'm not worth the effort that it will take to be set free from the deliberating grip of unforgiveness.

No longer will I settle for anything less than a pure authentic forgiveness process that will guide me on my journey to complete restoration and wholeness.

THAT TUESDAY MORNING, I CHOSE TO BE FREE!!!

Beloved, I know you're thinking... that's good for me, but I don't know your story,

...your hurt

...your disappointment

...or even the pain that you have experienced by the actions of someone else.

And you know what? You're right!

But what I do know...is that the same God that lovingly rescued and delivered me from the grip of unforgiveness desires to do the same for you.

What I do know... is that God was present with me right during every offense, every situation and circumstance that I've endured in my life and He is right there with you too.

What I do know... is that God wants to give you His liberating gift of forgiveness and release you from the shackles of unforgiveness.

What I do know... is that He loves you unconditionally, and that He truly wants you to operate in the freedom that forgiveness brings. More than anything I want that for you too.

What I do know... is that if you operate in forgiveness, what you would gain from your obedience, would far outweigh what you have lost by being disobedient and holding on to the unforgiveness.

Offering forgiveness to someone who has offended you is difficult and truly not for the faint at heart. It's a process that takes time to truly work through the journey in a healthy way. You may not ever get the response or apology you are expecting and rightfully speaking even deserve. Especially if the person is not around or may be deceased, and you aren't

IMAGINE ME

able to work it out with them in the natural. But regardless of the circumstances, God still expects for us to forgive them, so we can be released from the grip of unforgiveness in the process.

I wouldn't dare say that offering forgiveness to someone who's hurt you will be easy, but the good news is that God see all, knows all and is aware of it all and He is with you as your Vindicator. Therefore, you don't have to do it in your own power. You can exchange your strength for God's strength, in order to be able to offer forgiveness to your offender through the same Grace of God that you have received yourself.

Simply put, it all comes down to one single choice. Unfortunately, no one can make this choice for you, but you.

God has commanded us to choose life or death. His desire is that we would choose life. He has set before you this day, forgiveness, which represents life; and unforgiveness, which represents death. It's time for you to make a choice.

Would you dare believe God at His Word and exchange the familiar bondage of unforgiveness, for the liberating freedom offering forgiveness brings?

Would you dare step out in faith and trust God, as you choose life today and allow Him to do the rest?

Just know that I'm praying for you!

About Dana McCollum

Dana McCollum, is the proud mother of three amazing adults and affectionately known as "Grandma Dana" to her awesome grandkids. A Veteran of the United States Army, who has endured and OVERCOME many obstacles in her life to include; major illnesses, miraculous healing, tremendous grief and loss, widowhood, domestic violence, sexual assault, divorce, suicidal tendencies and much more.

Yet the Lord has delivered Dana from them all and has gifted her with a heart of compassion, smiles of hope and hugs of restoration, which she freely gives to those in her sphere of influence. Through her transparency others are often encouraged and challenged to look for God's presence in the midst of their own personal storms.

Dana has joyfully served the body of Christ and the community in various capacities for over 25 years. As an ordained Minister of the Gospel of Jesus Christ, a REAL Women Certified Facilitator and the Founder/Director of Transformed to Glory Ministries, a 501(c)(3) Ministry of Hope and Restoration, where the love of God is shown through action to inspire, encourage, and transform the hearts and lives of those we serve.

Her favorite scriptures are: Psalm 138:8: *For the Lord will perfect that which concerns me. Oh Lord, Thou mercy, endures forever. Do not forsake the works of your hands* and Philippians 4:13: *I can do all things through Christ who strengthens me.*

Contact

Email: transformedtoglory@gmail.com
Facebook: https://www.facebook.com/dana.mccollum

Dana's Acknowledgements

1 Thessalonians 5:18: *In everything give thanks for this is the will of God in Christ Jesus concerning you.* Thank you all from the bottom of my heart for allowing me to share my truth with you! I dedicate my chapter to anyone who can't imagine being set free from the bondage of unforgiveness. Today, I choose to believe with you and for you until your change comes!

MY FAITH AND GOD'S FAVOR

Stage 1

Imagine going to the OB-GYN for your yearly pap smear? You get undressed, put on that hospital gown, you sit there and WAIT for the doctor...

I was feeling fantastic, excited, and blessed! I had an excellent vacation in Jamaica with my sweetie in July! The ocean view cottage looked out at the beautiful turquoise blue waters. We walked right out to the beach in just a few steps. A few days after I returned from Jamaica my best friend Bertha called. I couldn't stop talking about my fabulously romantic trip! Bertha asked, "Are you ready to retire and travel?" I'd planned to work for 5 more years then retire. She said, "I need a roommate for a 10-day Hawaii vacation!" Bertha is my best, longest, and oldest friend. Thirty-seven years we've been friends! I quickly rearranged my budget, called her and said: "Yes, I'm in." The perfect trip to continue my yearlong birthday celebration. We met in

MY FAITH AND GOD'S FAVOR

Honolulu on November 11th. We stayed in Waikiki and toured the island for two days. The next seven days we cruised the islands of Hawaii, unbelievably breathtaking! The most beautiful God-made scenery I had ever seen! We sailed to the islands of Maui, Hilo, Kona, and Kauai. Delicious food is what we ate at the exclusive restaurants on board the ship, where you had to reserve tables in advance. This was my first time staying in a suite! Georgia, our personal assistant, took extraordinary care of us, she surprised me with birthday decorations and a party! A year of fun, relaxing, and exciting trips.

December 12th was just another day as I waited for Dr. S. I looked at the pictures from vacation and laughed. When she arrived, we chatted for a couple of minutes about my Jamaica and Hawaii trips. I laid back on the table, knees bent with my feet up in the stirrups, as she did her exams. After Dr. S. did the pap, I raised my arms above my head; and she examined my breast. Nothing different, she's been my doctor for 10 years. I was getting dressed, and she said, "We've talked about your breast before," I said, "Yes they've always been inverted," and smiled. I had just done my yearly mammogram 4 months ago in August. When she said, "I want you to see a breast surgeon," I thought it was a part of getting older; she probably recommended this for all women my age. On November 23, last month, I turned 60 years old. I looked great, ate healthy foods, and I felt great, I only weighed 120 pounds! I didn't think twice about a breast surgeon. As I got ready for bed; I felt something, a lump on my right breast. I thought to myself, Dr. S. felt the lump and

CAROL WRIGHT

didn't seem alarmed. I had nothing to worry about.

I looked over the list and called one of the breast surgeons she recommended the next day. This doctor wasn't accepting new patients until January. I made my appointment for January 12th. What're three more weeks to wait?

I continued with my day to day routines, getting up at 5:15 a.m.; driving to work in Washington DC; working at the U.S. Postal Service Headquarters. I enjoy my job, I have a passion for what I do, and that was helping others. I am a Sr. Executive Administrative Assistant to the Chief Information Officer! I have a great VP, and a great chief of staff, who I worked directly with. We have a smart, professional and strong team of individuals who work in the five departments in the CIO organization. On Sundays, it was time for church at New Life Pentecostal in Ruther Glen, VA! It's a one-hour drive on Sunday mornings. Sunday evenings, on the other hand, was a different story, often a two-hour drive after church. I grew up in Ruther Glen; I'm blessed to hear my cousin, Bishop Thomas Holmes sing and preach the Word! And did I say, HE CAN PREACH! When I left church, I spent time with my twin sister Carolyn; she is the nurturer of the family. I am the go-getter and the adventurous one. I left home after college and moved to Northern VA, got married to my childhood boyfriend June 5, 1981, a month before my Dad died. Being a wife lasted 10 years; free, single and independence is a lot more fun. Carolyn never left home; she quit her "good" government job to take care of Mom, until November 12,

MY FAITH AND GOD'S FAVOR

2006, when she passed away. Our family spent most of the day at the hospital with Mom and left around 10 p.m. I told my sisters I was spending the night at the hospital with Mom; my oldest sister Libby had stayed the past few nights, and Carolyn took wonderful care of Mom at home for years. I am so thankful I stayed that night. I laid next to Mom, and I whispered in her ear and reassured her, I would take care of the family. She closed her eyes and at 10:20 p.m. she took her last breath. Carolyn reminds me of Mom; she raised her two children, my nephew Aubrey, and niece Asia in the home we grew up in. I had 2 brothers, "Winnie," James, Jr., the oldest, who was 34, playing basketball in the gym, when he suffered a brain aneurysm and died; and Kirk my baby brother, they both had 2 sons. We are all 9 months apart in age, 3 of us were the same age for a couple of months each year. James Nelson and Annie didn't waste any time starting and raising a family. My dad was in the Army. We had a great childhood! My Mom was what we now call "a stay at home Mom." After my Dad returned from serving our country, he worked the night shift at McGuire Hospital in Richmond, VA. My Dad was always a strong provider. Me, I am like my Dad. I learned from his work ethic; he got up at 10 p.m. to drive to Richmond; he worked the midnight shift. I am blessed that I can provide for my niece and nephews. In 2016 Aubrey moved into his own apartment in Fredericksburg, VA, a major accomplishment for a young 26 years old male. Asia is more like me, outgoing, independent, and has been on her on since she left home for college in 2014. She is a senior at Old Dominion University. I am a proud Auntie!

CAROL WRIGHT

On January 1, 2018, I said to my sweetie, "I want to be engaged." We talked about how thankful we were to see 2018 and bring it in together. So many of our family and friends did not see another year. He suffered a mild stroke a few months ago and is blessed that God healed his body and he is talking and walking as if it never happened. To God be the glory! I said, yes that the what I want for 2018, to be engaged to him. I had no thoughts or plans of marriage. He is a widower and me a divorcee, and I still enjoy my independence. We all know everything happens for a reason, right? I asked him if he was okay with us being engaged, he laughed and said "YES!" My engagement ring came from JARED; it is a beautiful ring! Proverbs 18:22 says, he who finds a wife finds a good thing and obtains favor from the Lord. Even though I didn't wait for him to ask, I trust and believe the word of God, and he keeps on blessing me!

Stage 2

January 12th, the breast surgeon and assistant entered the room. Not knowing what to expect. I was still nonchalant about this appointment. The mammogram results less than 6 months ago were all normal. He asked a few questions and said, "I want to do an ultrasound," which he did. Then he said, "I want to do a biopsy." He asked if I wanted to schedule it and come back. I said, "No, let's do it now." Let me tell you; I am a big crybaby when I see a needle! I asked, "Are you going to put me to sleep?" He said, "No, I will numb the area." I said to myself, "Oh my god, I don't know if I can do this." But I knew I did not want to come back to have it done

MY FAITH AND GOD'S FAVOR

either. I did it, the biopsy, and yes, I cried like a baby. The assistant held my hand through the entire procedure. I went back for the test results on January 19th, a week later. I thought little about the biopsy during the week; I wasn't worried. There is a saying, or maybe it's a song, "if you pray don't worry, and if you worry, don't pray." I went into the same room I the biopsy done in, the doctor followed me and waited for his assistant to enter. He sat down on the stool, and she stood beside the door. He said, "The biopsy showed the lump was cancerous." He waited a couple of minutes; I assumed so I could digest what he said. He asked me, "Do you have any questions?" I said, "What stage would you say the cancer is?" He said, "Stage 1" He gave me a couple more seconds to digest that. He told me, "I want you to schedule an MRI." He said, "Once you get yourself together, see the receptions and make an appointment for the MRI." It's interesting because I didn't need to get myself together, I didn't cry; I didn't ask a lot of questions, and I didn't need to get dressed. I think I was in shock or disbelief. I didn't grasp what the doctor said. I went to the receptionist; she gave me a list of instructions. She, said, "you will get a call within 24 hours to schedule the MRI." She said, "You need to go to the imaging center where the mammogram was done and get a copy." She told me they needed the copy for their files. I said, "Excuse me," and she repeated everything. I walked out of the doctor's office, shaking my head, after the conversation with the receptionist. January 19th was Friday afternoon. I didn't get a call on Saturday or on Sunday, to schedule the MRI. I decided to get on the internet, and I googled the Cancer Treatment Centers of America (CTCA).

They had 24/7 assistance, so I called the toll-free number and spoke to a cancer treatment center advocate. When I told her the reason for my call, she said: "I'm sorry to hear you have been diagnosed with breast cancer." She gathered my information and told me she would have a scheduler call me the next day.

I was still waiting to hear from someone to schedule the MRI. I called the surgeon's office and said, "I thought someone was supposed to call me within 24 hours?" The receptionist said, "Oh you can call them." Again, shaking my head, I said, "really?" An hour later I got a call to schedule the MRI. The earliest they could see me was February 2. I told the assistant, "I've contacted the CTCA for a second opinion." As soon as I hung up, I got a call from the CTCA scheduler, and they asked, "How soon do you want to come in?" I said, "as soon as possible," the first available appointment was on January 31st. The next day the CTCA emailed me my entire two-day schedule with names and occupations of all the doctors I would see. I was relieved I could have everything done at one location.

Deuteronomy 31:6 says, be strong and of good courage, fear not, nor be afraid of them: for the Lord thy God, He it is that doth go with thee; he will not fail thee, nor forsake thee. I put in my leave request at work for 3 weeks. My mind was made up. I would stay in Philadelphia and do what I had to. I was not coming home until this cancerous lump was removed from my breast. (KJV)

MY FAITH AND GOD'S FAVOR

Stage 3

Over the next several days, I prepared to go to Philadelphia. Mentally, I was still in disbelief; I didn't tell my family. I didn't want them to worry, which is what they would have done. This was my journey, it was a test of my faith, and the only person I wanted with me was God. It was going to be okay; I trusted God. I say to myself, I would tell my family after meeting with the doctors at CTCA. I wanted my focus to be on God, my relationship with him; and to build one with the doctors. That would have been hard to do with family and friends around. I called my pastor, Tommy, on Wednesday, 5 days before I left to go to Philly. I told him I was diagnosed with breast cancer, I asked him to pray for me that night at Bible Study. The one thing I knew for sure is with pastor sending up prayers for me, everything was going to be alright. He's said before, you have to be careful who you ask to pray for you. On Sunday, January 28th the prayers continued during morning service, I was in the house of the Lord. I feel Gods presence! Pastor and I touched and agreed, God was in control. He sang There's a Miracle in This Room, With Your Name on It, by Tasha Cobbs. The Holy Spirit was moving, I felt his presence and everyone in the church felt it! I was blessed, I know God is a healer! Psalms 55:22 says, give your burdens to the Lord, and he will take care of you. He will not permit the godly to slip and fall (NLV). I laid my burdens downs and left them at the altar! I stopped by the house to see Carolyn before heading home. We eat and reminisced about back in the day. She and I, and my brothers, walked about a mile to meet Tommy and his sisters, Loretta and Zelda, at their house. We walked about 3 miles down Jericho road to church together on Sunday mornings. She and I laughed, I couldn't believe I use to sing in the choir. We agree, I can't sing. We all song in the young adult's choir. We sang this one song, "Glory Glory, Hallelujah, since I laid my burdens down; I feel better, so much better, since I laid my burdens down." We loved Sunday school and church, as kids we had no worries growing up. We had a good life, Tommy speaks about us growing up in his sermons often. "We were poor, but we didn't know it," we grew up in loving homes, with hard-working parents who loved us unconditionally. We got our butts whipped often when we acted up. Those were the good ole days! I decided to tell Carolyn I was heading to Philly next week for doctor's appointments. I said to her, "I have breast cancer." She said, "Why am I just hearing about this?" I told her I didn't want her worrying and getting sick. I said, "Gods got this." She said, "I'm going with you." I knew she would say that. I told her, I don't want anyone with me BUT GOD! She didn't understand why I didn't tell her and was going alone. I called my cousin Loretta who is a 5-year breast cancer survivor, I put her on speaker phone. I said, "I need you to be here to support Carolyn. I have breast cancer and I need you to be with her; talk to her and help her understand why I've made these decisions. I am going to be alright." Loretta was there for her and she encouraged Carolyn to trust, believe and have faith. I know my twin, she feels my pain and me hers; she would have worried herself sick about me. I trusted God and was not worried. I had no worries, God is a healer and would not leave or forsake me now; I knew he would be with me on this journey.

MY FAITH AND GOD'S FAVOR

I put my headsets on and I listened to my music as I took the 2-hour ride to Philadelphia from Union Station on January 30th. It was my first time on Amtrak, the trip was so peaceful. A driver from CTCA met me at Penn Station and took me to my hotel. CTCA made all the arrangements, I had no stress I felt they cared about me. The shuttle bus came every hour to take patients to and from the hotel to the CTCA.

Everyone is so nice, and I was treated like one of the family. I met with a dedicated team of doctors, my own, a primary care, surgeon, reconstructive, radiologist, oncologist, and genetics, as scheduled and a chiropractor, physical and occupational therapist after I made the decision to have the surgery on my 3rd day. Where else can you see all these doctors in one location? I went from one appointment to the next. They were all waiting for me, I felt like they already knew me. Each one was well informed, they had already reviewed my chart by the time I went in to see them. Very organized team! They had answers to all my questions.

After seeing all the doctors scheduled on my first day, my surgeon asked me, "Carol what do you want to do?" Based on all the doctors' opinions and the 3D mammogram he scheduled that did not detect the lump. I said to Dr. S., "I'm not having reconstructive surgery." Then I told him, I am having a double mastectomy, because if the mammogram did not detect the lump in my right breast, it's possible I could have one in my left. He said, "I think that's a good idea." I said, "I'm not taking any chances, remove both breasts; I only going through this once." He asked me, "When do you want to have the surgery?" I said, "Tomorrow," then I thought about it, "No let's not have it tomorrow, its super bowl weekend; Philadelphia is playing, and I want to enjoy the game!" I told him I was in Philadelphia for a reason and they were going to win because I was here. Dr. S. laughed, looked at his schedule and said, "what about Monday, February 5th?" I said, "Monday it is." He promised me he would not be up to late partying and enjoying the super bowl.

I got on an earlier shuttle and arrived early to CTCA. I sat in the waiting room relaxing, listening to gospel music on my phone, before my surgery. I called my pastor, Bishop Holmes and asked him to pray for and with me? We prayed and agreed! God is still in control, He was going to perform a miracle, please guide the surgeon's hands, there is healing in the name of Jesus, I would be healed in Jesus Name. I woke up in recovery a few hours later. I sat in bed, the nurses asked, "how do you feel", I said, "I felt fine." My sister, called around 5 p.m., and fussed at me, "Why didn't you call to let us know you were okay?" I had given the receptionist instructions to call my family. Not sure what happened to my message. Carolyn could hear in my voice that I was good, she wanted me to send her a picture, so she could see for herself. I laughed!

Dr. S. came by at 6 p.m. to check on me, he said the surgery went well, it was 2 ½ hours long and my stitches looked good. He said, "You will be released tomorrow." I said I could stay another day, just in case. He asked, "Are you in any pain?" I said, "No", he told me I would be going home.

MY FAITH AND GOD'S FAVOR

The next day I relaxed on the 2 p.m. train from Penn to Union Station. My good friends Gail and Ron met me at the train station. From the CTCA driver, to the train attendees, and Ron, I didn't have to lift a finger. I was home and in bed by 6 p.m. One day after having a double mastectomy, it's was hard to believe! Early, Wednesday morning, Carolyn, my cousin Loretta and her brother, Tommy who is my Pastor, were on their way to make sure I was okay and to help me out. Tommy worked at Reagan National Airport and dropped them off at my house for a few days. I called my sister's cell to see if they were on their way. She asked, "How do you feel?" I said, "I feel so good I can't stand myself!" They all laughed, but I was serious, I had no pain what so ever. I did not look like what I had been through. That was evident when Carolyn and Loretta walked through my front door. They couldn't believe, I was up, dressed, faced made up, and greeted them with a giant smile. I laughed and said, "I sent you all the pictures from my room yesterday after surgery." Well, it looks like I only sent the picture to Tommy, so he stood back and laughed at us. They cooked for me, they cleaned the kitchen, washed clothes and took very good care of me. I enjoyed their company, but I told Tommy to pick them up on Thursday. On his way home after he got off from work. They said I kicked them out...I did!

Stage 4

I went back to Philly on February 19th, for my follow-up appointments. When Dr. S. was ready to remove the drain tubes inserted in my chest, right under the area where I use to have breast, I said, "It's not going to hurt is it? I don't like pain." He said, "I don't either, I'll count to three," "one." I took a deep breath and it was out on the count of one. I laugh about it now! The doctors are so good, I never experienced any pain. He told me I was cancer free! My Oncologist, Dr. A. explained the different types of treatments plans and explained the pathology report. I agreed to a Genomics test to see how aggressive the cancer was. The test would be ready in about 30 days, I'll be back for my next appointment then. I stopped by my job when I got to DC and gave my VP and manager and update. They saw my joy, my VP said, "You are not coming back, are you?" I couldn't help but be happy and thankful, look at what the Lord has done for me. I was just told I was cancer free. I told her no, I didn't think I was coming back to work.

Stage 5

A friend called, she asked if she could give my information to a coworker who was just diagnosed with breast cancer. When I told her and other friends, I had breast cancer, I asked them not to tell others. I was the only one who could tell my story and I wanted friends and family to hear it from me. I said, "Sure, give her my cell number." I asked, "Who is it?" I couldn't believe it, it was my friend Connie. I didn't wait for her to call me, I called her. I asked if we could meet for lunch or dinner to talk. I came to HQ and picked her up and we went to lunch in the park. I told her my story and experience at the CTCA. Before we finished lunch, we called and made her an appointment at the CTCA. I told her I would go with

MY FAITH AND GOD'S FAVOR

her if she wanted me to. When I got home, I took a picture of my schedule and texted the information to her. She has the same team of doctors.

A few days later, I decided to reach out to family and friends through Facebook and Instagram. I wanted my family to know I had breast cancer and to share information with them. By sharing my story, I found out that at least 10 family members had cancer. I would have done the genetic testing if I had known this before my surgery. My nephew Andre died of cancer at age 32, after a 10-year battle. My aunt and several cousins' loss their battle cancer also. We have to educate the next generation in our family, so they are aware of the effects of cancer in our family.

I contacted my Human Resources Shared Service Center and requested my retirement annuity and paperwork. I hadn't been to work in 2 months. I 've enjoyed the time off, I needed it to strengthen my body and to continue my very personal relationship with God. I am so blessed! God prepared me for cancer! I thank him for touching my body with cancer and not my twin sister. Gratitude is my attitude and I have an attitude of gratitude with unspeakable joy. My steps were ordered, God had a plan for me, and he doesn't make any mistakes. I trusted and believed. He is a faithful God, He was with me on this journey and will walk along beside me through it all. Hebrews 13:5, Let your conversation be without covetousness; and be content with such things as ye have: for he hath said, I will never leave thee, nor forsake (KJV).

CAROL WRIGHT

On March 25, 2018, I was baptized again and rededicated my life to God. I will bless the Lord at all times: his praise shall continually be in my mouth. My soul shall make her boast in the Lord; the humble shall hear thereof and be glad. O magnify the Lord with me and let us exalt his name together. I sought the Lord, and he heard me, and delivered me from all my fears. Psalm 34 (KJV).

My life has been changed!

#cancerfreein30day

What a difference 30 days can make!

How I kicked cancers Ass in 30 days!

About Carol Wright

My name is Carol Nelson Wright, I am a 6-month breast cancer survivor.

My twin sister Carolyn raised her 2 children in the home we grew up in and gave up her government job to take care of our mom. She's my hero! My brother Kirk is also incredible, He's a hard worker and he and his wife live life like it's golden.

I'm the adventurous one, who moved to Northern Virginia to begin my career after college.

I retired April 30, 2018, after 37 years of federal service. The next chapter in my life started in Raleigh, NC, on June 5, 2018. I'm excited to see what God has planned for me.

Contact

#MyFaithandGodsFavor
#Cancerfreein30days
Facebook: MsCarol Wright
Email: msc54u2@gmail.com

Carol's Acknowledgements

None of this would have been possible if not for the Lord on my side. I give God all the praise and the glory. I would like to acknowledge my twin sister Carolyn who has always been right by my side through thick and thin. She feels my pain and I feel hers; that's the closeness and bond we've shared since birth. I love you so much. To my brother Kirk, a strong, determined man, who has always worked hard to support his family. I admire that so much in you. You will continue to be blessed because of the man you are.

My cousin, Tommy, thank you for teaching me the Word of God at New Life Pentecostal Church. God has blessed you abundantly with favor because of your faithfulness. I know that I'm blessed because of you, our church family, and God. Thank you for praying with me just before I went into surgery. I know God heard your prayer request for a miracle. I am a living witness!

To all my family and friends (you know who you are), thank you for your support. I love you guys. I pray that God will continue to bless you and your families! Have faith and let the Lord direct your footsteps, as He has done for me, in Jesus' name, I pray, Amen!

SILENT SCREAMS

No one really knows when mother's troubles began. Some say that she was always a precocious child, happy at times, and quite strong willed.

Born the middle child, mother was named after her paternal grandmother, Grace Beatrice, to good Southern Baptists folks who affectionately called her Gracie.

Mother was raised on a farm in Southeastern Virginia with plenty of fresh air, sunshine, and rolling meadows.

Some say that she was never the same after she was raped at sixteen, by a relative. No one called sexual abuse "RAPE" back then. Not in the South. Not in the 1960s.

No one paid for Gracie's loss of innocence. No one believed her. No one vindicated her. However, Gracie paid. Gracie bore the shame, the blame, the pain, and the guilt her entire life.

SILENT SCREAMS

Unable to move forward in a small town, resilient, and strong-willed, Gracie found the strength to move forward. It was the late 1960s and everyone was "finding themselves".

Mother moved to Washington, DC, and secured a job as a secretary with the federal government. Mother had bounced back and even found someone to love.

Mother said that she noticed him in the cafeteria. He was wearing a brown suit. She said to herself, "That Abe Spencer sure is a fine-looking man."

It was the spring of 1969. My father in his 40s, a Korean War veteran, a gentle, southern man, who never thought he would settle down because city women were just too complicated.

My parents fell in love, got married, and in the late summer of 1971, I was born. and all was right with the world.

Some say Mother's troubles began when my father passed away. My father suffered and died from a respiratory disease called pleurisy, which is not very common today.

My father departed this world Spring of 1975, a few months shy of my 4th birthday. My mother buried him in that same brown suit he wore when she first laid eyes on him.

Soon after my father's passing, my mother suffered a nervous breakdown of which she never recovered.

KENYETTA MILLS

Mother was not able to bounce back from my father's death. I figure her heart had been broken one too many times.

I can remember when I was a young child. Mother's eccentricities became stranger and stronger. Often times we would live from hotel to hotel on the run from her imagined persecutors. Then there were times mother would hear voices and talk to people who were not there.

Sometimes mother would hide me in the closet to keep me safe from whatever strange manifestations she was experiencing.

Mother's chaotic world became normal to me during my childhood, and despite all of the nonsense and drama, I still clung to her and loved her very much.

In the mid-1980s mother was diagnosed with paranoid schizophrenia.

Frequently on and off her medication, and in and out of abusive relationships, Mother would attempt suicide at least twice, overdosing on sleeping pills. Once, I even found her and called the paramedics.

It is remarkable how resilient children are. I went to school. I excelled in my studies. I was vibrant, social, and outgoing. Yet, I came home to a nightmare every day. Mother's illness made her moody and unpredictable. There was never enough food, love, attention, or affirmation. Life was rough most of the time. However, when it was good it was very good.

Though I never knew what normal was, I often cried myself to sleep hoping to one day have a normal life.

Mother was a very attractive woman. After my father died, she looked for someone to fill his void, but she never found love. Mother was a magnet to abusive men. She spent most of my youth chasing after one "no-good-man" after the other. Mother was in and out of more abusive relationships than I could count. All while I longed for her love, but rarely received it.

Mother would give birth to three more children. The youngest was born on a cold January night. Mother, (off her meds at the time) went into labor, and I helped her give birth to a baby girl on our living room sofa.

I wrapped my baby sister in a towel and kept her warm until the paramedics arrived. I was thirteen years old.

The next day, Social Services came and took us away again. Due to Mother's mental state, she lost her paternal rights. My baby sister was placed up for adoption. I would not be reunited with her for eighteen years.

My younger brothers and I would spend our childhood in and out of foster care. In addition, Mother was in and out of psych wards – while on and off her medication.

Throughout most of my formative years, Mother was my big secret because mental illness was such a stigma in society.

It was not until I read Stormie Omartian's book, "Just Enough Light For The Step I'm On", which details her traumatic childhood, that I came to terms with my own past.

I can appreciate a teacher who is not afraid to show their scars because it gives me the courage to show mine. Here I am before you today showing you my scars because God never wastes a hurt.

It is still very hard for me to share about the night Mother decided that she had enough of this world. In a nursing home, unable to breath on her own, Mother pulled out her trachea, and asphyxiated. With a "do not resuscitate" on file there was nothing the nursing staff could do. I screamed. I begged. I cried as I watched mother suffocate. When her gasping for air ceased, Mother was pronounced brain dead.

While Mother lay unconscious in hospice care, God gave me four months to pray over her, sing over her, tell her how much I loved her, and say all the things I could never say to her due to our strange relationship. Mother passed away leaving her troubles behind on May 15, 2017, on Monday, the day after Mother's Day.

I truly believe mother entered God's kingdom and finally

received the peace she had searched for all her life but could never find.

Some people are not born free in this life. Some people try to find freedom and never find it. For some death comes to set them free.

I can remember the hospice nurse calling to check on me months after Mother's passing. She knew the struggles Mother had with mental illness.

I told the nurse how hard it was for me to get used to normal. No weird phone calls in the middle of the night. No tells of strange manifestations. No drama. No chaos. Just normal. The Hospice nurse replied, "Kenyette you are free too. It is okay to have normal."

I am still grieving the loss of my mother. I grieve over the pain Mother was in. I grieve over the things we were never able to do together. I grieve over the sad life she lived and the tragic way in which she died.

There are some things in life you just do not get over. Yet, God gives you the strength to get through.

There is not a day that goes by that I do not think about my mother. Yet at the same time, I feel like a person who has been set free from a life-long prison sentence.

The little girl that would often cry herself to sleep, hoping for a normal life, is finally free too.

If you are struggling today coping with a loved one's mental illness, you need an anchor to carry you through the turmoil, to carry you through the chaos. That anchor is Jesus Christ. You can know Him today! You do not have to suffer in silence. There is help. God hears our silent screams.

About Kenyette Mills

Burning with Passion For God

I am a "burning one." My goal is to reach, teach, and unleash other "burning ones". I am the author of "Atomic Prayers: Combating Cancer through Prayer" and "From Here to There- Vision Board Workshop".

I am in love with a Jewish man. His name is Jesus. He is the Messiah. He is the hope for the entire world.

The word Seraphim means "burning ones" or "nobles". Their primary duty is to glorify God in pure and radiant love. Their eternal song is, "Holy, holy, holy is the LORD God almighty; who was, and is, and is to come."

In this latter-day revival there is an emergence of an ancient prophetic stream to raise up burning-ones, to refresh the weary warrior, to set ablaze those in slumber, and to ignite a prayer-movement.

Contact

Kenyette9671@yahoo.com

WEEPING MAY ENDURE FOR A NIGHT

"*Weeping may endure for a night, but joy comes in the morning.*" I had read, studied, preached and heard this passage of scripture for a vast majority of my life. When people would come to me with their issues and problems, the resolve that I would give, was this scripture found in Psalms 30:5. I believed it with all of my heart. I believed that tough times did not last, but tough people do.

While I still believe, my understanding is totally different. Experience was definitely my teacher. Within two years I had to find a way to live while it felt like I was actively dying. My marriage had died. This death would become contagious to every other part of me. My passion died, my will died, my mind died, my heart died. The only thing still alive in me was my purpose, and the only reason that my purpose stayed alive was because I did not know it, and I suppose it was safe because it was still a mystery to me.

WEEPING MAY ENDURE FOR A NIGHT

I walked away thinking to myself, oh the agony of suffering an injury and having to endure the pain over a year later. I was working a private health care case and my client was suffering from broken ribs. He had broken his ribs some time ago and did not allow the sufficient time to heal. In doing so, he reinjured his ribs. He would often speak of how his pain and injuries would hinder him from doing the things that he once loved doing. He couldn't climb a ladder and finish painting the ceilings. He couldn't bend over or kneel to replace baseboards or start a lawn mower or lay carpet or tile. As I listened to him speak, I could hear the frustration in his voice, and the loss of pride in his eyes. I took notice of how low and broken he spoke while holding his head down in the posture of defeat and disappointment. It was then that I was lead to study broken ribs and the recovery time.

Broken ribs are defined as a fracture or break in one or more bones making up the ribcage. Broken ribs can heal in a month or two. People with broken ribs can treat their injuries at home by applying ice and resting properly and taking pain medications. Basically, it just takes time and a willingness to follow the treatment plan. In that moment everything was beginning to come together. After almost 5 years, my marriage met its resolve. All the lies, stress, disappointments and unfaithfulness had met its mark. In the final blow, anger and rage came flooding over me. When he decided not to come home until late in the midnight hour and thought he owed me no explanation of where he was, it angered me even more. I had been having thoughts and instincts told me there was someone else, but I had no proof. I questioned and begged for a response. His only answer was he was done with our marriage and family.

Out of rejection, anger and hurt, I began to rattle off five years of repressed feelings and emotions. I was like an erupting volcano. The peace that I had held for so long, was now becoming a distant memory. All I could think about was the lies that I never confronted him with. All the times I thought we were in a financial struggle, only to find out that he had more than enough to meet the needs of the family he vowed to provide for. The way he would treat my children when he thought I was not looking or unaware. Listening to the voice of others. He abandoned me and my children to become one of the cool guys. The cheerleader in his ear was louder than the team we built. After this he told me that me and my children had to leave the house. He wanted us gone. Stating that our names were not on the lease. I knew legally that he could not make me, or my children leave, and at first, I told him to bring his best shot because I was prepared for the fight. Then I heard the voice of the Lord tell me to walk away naked. I fell to the floor and just began to cry, and even questioning God. Why was this even happening to me.

In the beginning he was the perfect gentleman. He opened my car door, gave me forehead kisses, became a father figure to my children, praying for us as a family and many other things that gave me reason to have confidence in him as a man. After about the 3rd year of marriage, I encountered the real man. The representative could not weather the storm. I was not a perfect wife, but I was a good

WEEPING MAY ENDURE FOR A NIGHT

wife and I did the best I could, and I had every intention on fighting for my family and marriage. I chose to support him even when the decisions he made did not benefit us as husband and wife or family. Covering him at all cost and losing myself in the process. But I was doing all of this from a broken place, as a broken rib. All I had done was just mask the obvious and what I was really doing was protecting an image.

What I had perceived as growth was just an infection and the poison from the bite of the enemy and the infection was creating a mirage in the middle of the desert I found myself in. I was broken, I was angry, I was crushed. I was a broken rib. I had been broken for some time and it was finally slow walking me down. I buried myself in work and tried my best not to feel the pain, but it was beginning to show. I had stopped eating. I lost over 45 pounds in a matter of weeks. I just worked and slept and prayed. Not conscious of what I was doing to myself, my mind had convinced my body to die. I found myself in a place where I did not want to keep going. Then I had days when I didn't even believe that my life mattered and was worth living. I was tired of going through the same things over again. I was tired of the disappointments, and I was tired of the pain. Pain was something that I knew well, and it was also something that I knew I would have to endure. Didn't have the understanding why but, I knew it had to be done.

I couldn't take Advil this time and have the pain subside. I had to do nothing short of walk through this valley and surely death was with me. I was at work one night, and the stress and depression had finally thrown its final blow. I was on the only hall in the building that didn't have a camera. My head began to spin, and my body had become weak to the point where I had begun to stumble trying to keep my balance. I felt my knees buckling, and I began to go down. On the way to the cold hard floor, I heard the voice of the Lord speak to me and say, "He's not worth it daughter!" I tried to crawl to the bathroom, thinking if I could just get some cold water on my face, I would be alright. I could still hear the voice of Christ ministering to me saying "I am with you always, even unto the end of the world."

I replied, "Even in this?"

"Even in this daughter," He said.

I just laid on the bathroom floor and began to pray and cry. I had to repent and pray some more. I felt the presence of the angels on the floor with me, strengthening and covering me. I knew that a hard road was in front of me, but I also knew that it would be life-altering, and it was a road that I needed to travel and overcome.

More than anything, I knew that my life was worth living. In my dying moment, I decided to live. I knew I had to forgive. I knew that I had to let go of the pain that had crippled me and had become such huge part of my life. Pain will always have a dwelling place wherever anger and bitterness and unforgiveness reside. Before we can forgive we must acknowledge the offense and know what we are forgiving. I fault myself with never allowing myself time to fully heal in the past. I would go through some hard things in this life I live and

WEEPING MAY ENDURE FOR A NIGHT

instead of dealing with the issues and acknowledging the pain, I would push it under the rug and force myself to get over it, I never took the time to examine my heart and the feelings. I never took the time to make sure I was ok. There was even a time when I thought that I deserved the bad things that would happen to me. I began to find pleasure in other things that would help me forget about the pain I had been going through. And it worked for a long time. Until I would be faced with the same issue again. Then the old wound would reopen, and I would have to deal with the present pain and the old pain. Instead of overcoming the obstacles that would afflict me, I gave them a dwelling place in my head and my heart. I had to forgive myself for not loving myself enough to heal.

We become a target for rejection and abandonment as well as low self-esteem and many other things when we walk around day to day wearing band-aides on wounds that need stitches. My road to healing and recovery was a very hard one for me. I had days where I cried from sun up to sun down. I had days where I didn't want to go on anymore. Then I had days where I didn't feel anything at all. It was those days that I thought I was finally healing and wouldn't have to feel another day of pain, only to wake up the next morning in my bed all alone, missing the life that I had once knew. Anger and resentment would flood my soul all over again. Shame began to be a part of the garment that I put on every day. It was as if someone had put my pain on repeat and played it all day. That someone was me. I was so broken and hurt I didn't know how to live. I was stuck in a place of questioning

REGINA HARRELL

"How could he just throw me away like that? Was I not worthy of a fight to the finish?"

Then forgetting all of the things that lead to such a horrible event, I began blaming myself for everything. I should have done this and that differently. I was trying to figure out ways to live and survive in pain. Pain is the one thing I have known all my life. It's the one thing that I knew how to maneuver through. But this time God had enough of me doing things my way. We as people, especially women, will hold on tight to the things that God himself is trying to rip away from us. That displays a lack of trust in Him. I was tired of being sad and I was tired of fighting against the will of God. I remember falling to my knees in the middle of the bedroom floor, crying out, "Lord, if this is a fire that I must walk through, I will, but please don't leave me at the mercy of man." While in prayer, I could still hear Christ tell me to walk away naked. No answers, no house, no car and no money. And on top of that I had to forgive. But the Lord promised to take care of me and my children. And that he did. He opened doors and showed favor when I went to apply for a place to stay. He showed favor when I walked on the car lot and drove off with no money down. He showed favor when I receive a promotion and raise on my job. He was taking care of me and all he asked of me in this moment was to forgive. That was a very hard thing for me to do at first. I had lost too much to just forgive. But, I had everything to gain.

Holding a grudge was nothing more than a way to hold on to something that was already dead. Refusing to forgive was

WEEPING MAY ENDURE FOR A NIGHT

how I continued to hit the replay button on pain. Unforgiveness was the door that anger, depression and feelings of worthlessness walked through and set up camp in my heart and my head. In my brokenness, the only other option was to forgive. I had to lose the anger and embrace the passion and love of Christ. There is nothing worse than forgiving someone who thinks they have done nothing wrong. But I did it anyway. I picked up the phone and called him after not speaking to him for months. He didn't answer the call, so I emailed him. I told him that whatever pain I caused him, and for every short-coming as a wife, I was sorry, and I repent. I told him that I forgive him for it all. Hitting send was one of the hardest things I ever had to do. But I did it anyway. And although my heart was still broken, I was free.

I was laughed at, talked about and lied on. Never once did I defend myself. I held on to the promises of God, that he was faithful to perfect those things concerning me. I knew that vengeance was still His and He would repay. Through one of the most painful times in my life, I encountered the true love of God. That's something that would have been impossible if I continued to let bitterness and unforgiveness occupy my head and heart space. I forgave people that hurt me, and I also forgave myself for allowing myself to be walked on by those who were never worthy of my presence in the first place. When you settle for less in your life you will always receive lessor of the greater things you could have. Settling for less, leaves so much room for things to do you more harm than good.

I forgave because I wanted to live. Once a person walks out of your life, don't allow them the space in your mentality to contaminate your future. Their role in your life, no matter how great or small, is now over. You must love yourself enough to move on. My heart was still hurting but through forgiveness, I could now receive beauty for my ashes. My pain was now in the hands of one greater than I. I still had my good days and bad days, and that was ok. I was allowed to have those moments, because it was those moments that would usher me into my healing.

Now that I had forgiven, I was free to heal. To forgive someone is to cancel the debt or offense committed. But it does not cancel the pain of the offense. Time and healing does this. Now that forgiveness had taken place, I was free to heal. My recovery could begin. Healing is a process as well as an experience. When allowed the time to do so, healing will allow you the ability to become sound and healthy again. Where going through the process of healing, I had to be mindful of my surroundings as well as the people that were around me. Envisioning myself as an open wound, tender to the touch and exposed for all to see, I knew that I could not allow the offenders to bring offense again.

I'm reminded of the time shortly after I left my home, I ended up in the hospital. I thought I was having a heart attack but turns out it was anxiety. After being in the hospital for 3 days, upon my release, the doctor gave me a treatment plan. By the time he gave me the long list of do's and don'ts, I was thinking to myself, I don't need all of this. And in the same

WEEPING MAY ENDURE FOR A NIGHT

breath, I told myself that there was no need in coming to the hospital if I was not going to follow the treatment plan. One of his main directives, was to stay away from the things that were triggering my anxiety. He was telling me to stay away and all I wanted to do was call on the very people and persons that had depleted me. Telling myself that if I did not have what it takes to make a simple phone call, then I had not really forgiven. That was not the case at all. I forgive, but you don't get another opportunity to pour salt in my open wounds. Not only did I have to follow the doctor treatment plan, but I also had to follow the treatment plan that Christ had laid out for me.

To be made whole, I needed first to desire wholeness. I had to want to made whole. In the 5th chapter of John, we read of a man that suffered from an infirmity for 38 years. When Jesus saw him, he already knew his condition and he had been this way for a long time. Then he asked him, wilt thou be made whole? The man answered him with an excuse, as if he had to explain and justify why he was in this condition for so long. He answered him saying that he had no one to put him in the pool when the water is troubled. He further explains that while he is coming to the pool. People step in front of him. Jesus said to the man, Rise, take up your bed and walk. The word of God was and still is my treatment plan. I used to feel the need to explain myself and situation, when all I really needed was a sure yes, to the question of whether or not I wanted to be made whole.

We have to get past the place where we desire to explain

ourselves and justify our actions. No one is allowed in the recovery room while I heal. That's it, no explanation needed. After establishing the desire, now we must have faith. For faith is the substance of things hoped for, but the evidence of things not seen. In the midst of brokenness, there is no evidence that your heart will be made new, there is no evidence that it will even beat again. There is no evidence that you will ever love again. There is no evidence that the dark clouds will roll away. But our hope is in the Word and promise of Christ. Our faith and our trust have a right to be there.

There will be days where your faith in people and their humanity will be shattered. We will come to a place where we resent those who walked away and shut out those that have honest and pure motives, and prevent them from coming in. Being abandoned and left alone in any situation is a painful place. It is a hurt that cannot be explained. I believe that we have the right to be frustrated where we do not see a return of the investment of love and appreciation invested. Especially when it comes from someone that vowed to honor, protect and provide for, in sickness and in health, for better or for worse. While having the temporary right and desire to be frustrated and irritated, we owe it to ourselves not to remain in this place. Become frustrated and irritated to the point that something beautiful comes from the collide. Something like a diamond, ruby or a pearl. Have you ever noticed how certain things came together after people walked away from you? Have you noticed that as you healed, your vision and perspective changed for the better

WEEPING MAY ENDURE FOR A NIGHT

and you began to see the fruit of your labor? Your promise and destiny are not coupled with the things and people who left you, although they do play a role, possibilities do not end with those that abandoned you. The role some play is labeled as a roadblock. They hindered you from your next place, while the pain and disappointment will motivate you through their absence. It all was necessary. You may not see it now, but you will grow to be thankful for the walkaways.

About Regina Harrell

Pastor Regina Harrell is a native of Winston Salem, NC. She is the daughter of Rev. Wade and Rebecca Butler. A nurturer of the people of God by nature, she has professionally worked in the field of healthcare for 20 years obtaining licenses and certifications to bring substance to her passion. Pastor Harrell surrendered her life to Christ in August 1994 and has continued to serve faithfully refusing to come down. Pastor Harrell has functioned in multiple capacities within the Body of Christ from Armor Bearing to Evangelism. She stood as the Assistant Pastor of The Kingdom Center International Ministry and in 2011 she founded Myrtle Tree Ministries which was the foundation of what she would later be used to cultivate many lives.

Pastor Harrell is the Pastor of The Recovery Place in Winston Salem, NC. She launched H2TKO- Heels, Harley's and The Kingdom Outpour in October 2016 which is an organization by which she has continued to come outside of the box to embrace women from all walks of life. She sits under the honored covering of The Redemption Church where the leaders are Pastor David and First Lady Victoria Venable.

Pastor Harrell flows in a powerful, yoke-destroying anointing from which flows healing and deliverance. Her voice shatters atmospheres and she is uniquely one of a kind in Christ Jesus! She truly has a heart for people and seeks to see them free in every area of their lives. She preaches, teaches and lives the Gospel of Jesus Christ. Without a doubt, she loves the Lord and seeks His perfect will for her life. She is quoted saying "In my life, I know loss, I know pain and suffering, I know failure...through these things I encountered the unwavering and unconditional love and power of Jesus Christ."

Pastor Harrell is the only daughter of seven siblings and the proud mother of four sons. She finds solace in Psalms 91. *"He that dwelleth in the secret place of the most high, shall abide under the shadow of the Almighty."*

Contact

Email: recoveryourlife@outlook.com
Instagram: @ladyrecovery
Facebook: Regina W. Harrell

WHO ME?

It always brings tears to my eyes when I watch awards shows. Seeing the nominee who has no idea or thinks that he/she will hear their named called. Then it happens. They hear their name, there's the sheer look of amazement, the shock on their face, their hands covering their mouth; as it drops open. They begin looking around in utter disbelief, as if to get another's approval; asking with their eyes, "Who me... Did you know?" The tears, the hugs, the slow walk to the stage, while trying to gather their thoughts and emotions together, because they have no speech prepared. "What will I say? Who I will thank? I hope I don't forget anyone or make a fool of myself."

January 10, 2009 was kind of like that for me. Let me explain. It was announced two weeks before the event was to occur, that the choir would have its first annual CCA awards, which stands for Commitment, Consistency and Accountability, by our church's Minister of Music, Tangie Rowe. She was a medium height, brown-skinned woman, who is an awesomely

WHO ME?

anointed musician, and choir director. As she explained what the event was about, she indicated she wanted to recognize individual choir members, and show her appreciation to the choir as a whole, for their service to God, and the music ministry. The top awards would go to the man and woman who had been the most committed, consistent and accountable. My stomach had butterflies and my heart sank, as I thought, and chuckled to myself, "Well I know I won't be getting anything. I might as well just show up, get something to eat, and be happy for the folks that win."

As I pulled up to the fellowship hall, I pondered the thought in my mind, "Maybe...just maybe . . . I have always been committed, consistent and accountable. Snap out of it. It's not going to happen." I was thinking about how I had recently just come back to the choir. I had left for various reasons over the years - twice being pregnant. This reason was much different. I thought I was removing myself, from the choir, but it was actually God removing me. We had five choir directors, before Tangie came, and some choir members over the years had taken ownership of something that did not belong to them, which was God's ministry. But at the time I did not recognize that I was one of them.

As I entered the building, I took a deep breath, put on my happy church face--the one we all have when we really don't want anyone to know what's going on inside our hearts. I could smell the aroma of pasta, and garlic bread. I could hear the chatter, laughter, and excitement blaring as I walked down the long hall to the main room. As I crossed the threshold, with a smile, "Wow! She really put a lot into this." I said to myself, as I panned the room. It was beautiful. The tables were decorated with white plastic coverings, centerpieces, and each table had a place setting in front of a chair. The front of the room was set with microphones, keyboards, and a drum set for the praise and worship group that was going to minister to us in song. As I worked the room, saying my "hellos", kissing, and hugging folks, I still could not shake this feeling in the pit of my stomach. I didn't quite understand why I was feeling this way. I had already prayed and resolved within myself that I could be happy for whoever won, and that my service to God didn't depend on accolades from other people.

I found a seat, and without sitting down, grabbed a plate, and went to get some of the pasta dish that I had smelled the moment I entered the building. After I got my food, I made my way back to my table. I sat not far from other people, but kind of by myself. As I sat waiting for the event to begin, my mind flashed back to being in this very room April 11, 2008, at the Women's Ministry fellowship, apologizing, to Tangie asking for her forgiveness for not loving her past her faults, gossiping, and slandering her name to others in the church. See at the time, I did not realize that God was using her issues to show me mine.

The food was good. I had definitely bought my appetite as I went up for seconds, greeting others who had arrived after me, I noticed Minster Angie Williams. "Hey Angie, what's going on?" I asked as I hugged her and kissed her on the

WHO ME?

cheek. Minister Angie is a brown-skinned, fly-dressing, anointed woman, who can preach her tail off; she is also my accountability partner. "How did last night go?" she asked. "Girrrl, I'm still in awe of what God did through me. He blessed. God did just what He said He was going to do." Because I had been obedient to God in forgiving Tangie, and did it publicly, He revealed that He was also calling me into the ministry on August 8, 2008. He further confirmed that calling the night before the awards, when I taught the women on "Obedience". How ironic, but that's how God does things sometimes.

The program began as Jackie Eudell, the Mistress of Ceremony of the evening, called us to order. Jackie is a beautiful, brown-skinned woman, with a smile that lights up a room. She greeted, and reminded us, of the reason for the event. She then introduced Carolyn Bowden and called her to the podium, to give the occasion, and the history of the choir. Carolyn is a light-skinned older woman, in her sixties, who doesn't look a day over fifty. She has a way of telling a story, one that keeps you engaged, and hanging on to her every word. That night however, my mind was still thinking on how God had taught me how to love his people the way He does. He had taught me to love people past their faults. Showing me how I had equated the things that were happening between Tangie and me, thinking that she was standing in the way of what God had declared in my life. But how was she to know? I never shared it with her.

How was she to know, that I couldn't sing my way out of a

paper bag. That it was God who told me to join the choir, and I was just fool enough to step out on faith, and believe Him? How was she to know that God had given me a vision, dreams, and called me to be a worship leader? How could I think that she and not God had control over my destiny? How was I to know that the prayers I had prayed for God to teach me to love His women, that He was using her to do it? How was I to know, that when God declares the end from the beginning, there is a middle, and I was smack dab in the middle of it. He was showing me things in me that I didn't know were there. He was breaking me and molding me for His use. And all the while I was asking God, "Who me? I didn't know that was there." Asking Him, "But God, how am I going to be a worship leader, and I'm not even in the choir." God was saying to me, "It has to be about Me. I'm teaching you to worship Me in spirit and in truth, not just in how well you sing, but worshipping Me from your heart in song. I'm working it out for your good, and My glory. Stop chasing after what only I can give you."

Jackie then called Tangie to the podium. It was now time for the awards to be given. My heart was in my stomach, pretty much where it had been all evening and now full of food to boot. Tangie said a few words of thanks, and how this evening came to be. "This first award is for the person who comes every first Sunday to sing with us from another church, and I want to recognize her for her faithfulness." She called "Kathy Williams." We all stood and applauded, as she made her way to the front, to receive her trophy. I thought, "Yeah, she deserves that, she has been coming for a while. I had

WHO ME?

forgotten she wasn't a member here", as I continued clapping for her. Well I made it through that one. I'm happy for her. Thank you, Lord! "Next I want to recognize this person for always being on point, sending out the music, and choir information." We all knew who she was talking about, before her named rolled off her tongue, "Regina Gray." "Yeah!" I said out loud, as I stood up to clap for her. She is good at what she does. "You go girl," I yelled out to her."

As we settled down Tangie, with a big smile on her face said "The next person I want to recognize will receive the CCA award. This person comes out, and sings every Sunday, even though he has been the only man for years; but he still comes out, and deals with us ladies anyway." We all laughed, everyone knew it was, Rick Walker, as he made his way to the front we all stood, clapped and chanted his name. "Wow! God this is not hard at all. I can do this," I thought, with a big smile on my face. We all sat down, as Tangie continued, "Last but not least, I want to recognize the woman of the CCA award." "Oh God, this is a little harder. I'm good." I said to myself, "You can do this, you can be happy for any woman in this room."

"This person has always been committed, consistent and accountable. She's here most times before I get here, putting out the chairs," Tangie continued.

"Ok," I thought, "who is she talking about?" She continued. "When the choir was going through, and we did not have many members, she called me, encouraged me, and gave me a word. She said, "Keep putting the chairs out, and watch God fill them." Then it hit me! She's talking about me, at the same time she called my name. I'm that nominee. The one who has no idea or thinks that he/she will hear her named called. It happened. I heard my name. With the sheer look of amazement, and the shock on my face, my hands covered my mouth as it dropped open, and I began looking around in utter disbelief; as if to get another's approval; asking with my eyes, "Who me?" "Did you know?" Then came the tears, the hugs, and the slow walk to the stage; trying to gather my thoughts, and emotions together, because I have no speech prepared. "What will I say? Who I will thank? I hope I don't forget anyone or make a fool of myself." Well it wasn't that dramatic, and there was no speech, thank God!

As I made my way to the podium, all I could think is, "God you are Awesome! I could never understand why You told me to call her, and tell her that, after I had left the choir. It didn't make sense to me then, but it was making perfect sense to me now." We hugged with a long embrace of genuine love for one another with our faces full of tears; tore up with the "Ugly Face." It has since then been our joke, when the Spirit hits us, "Ooh girl you really had the "ugly face" today." She whispered in my ear, "I love you girl." God had done it! I believed that this was her way of saying, "Chris, will you forgive me too?" In the same public way that I had asked for her forgiveness. God had healed our relationship, in a way I had never seen coming.

I'll never forget that day, and everything that lead up to it.

WHO ME?

For it has shaped and molded me, as I allowed God to build character in me, and make me fit for His use. I now understand why I had that pit- feeling in my stomach. It was the Holy Spirit, preparing me, and letting me know that I had been delivered from chasing what only He could give me. Although I still find myself, asking God the question, "Who me? I didn't know that was there," because God is not through with me yet.

About Chris Allen

His purpose for her life through His word, Jeremiah 1:1-9. As God confirmed in her, "Then the LORD reached out his hand and touched my mouth and said to me, "Now, I have put my words in your mouth." Since this time, she has been a mouthpiece and a vessel ready to be used for God's glory. It is her calling to encourage and to empower men and women of all ages to know who they are in Christ, and to know how much He loves them. It is her vision to see people develop a closer and more intimate relationship with Christ as they learn to live freely in the abundant life He died to give us.

Chris is the author of *Restoration Speaks ~ Speak Loud A Bible Study Devotional* and *Restoration Speaks ~ Speak Loud Journal*. She is also scheduled to release *Restoration Speaks ~ My Journey to Wholeness*, which will be released in February of 2019. She is a leader and Founder of Anointed Women in Chris, LLC (AWIC) ministry. AWIC has its own television show on the WBGR Gospel Network called AWIC TV "Experience It." Additionally, Chris has a flourishing entrepreneurship as a consultant for Traci Lynn Jewelry (Tracilynnjewelry.net/ChrisLovesBling) and Thrive (purpose4christ.thrive2point0.com).

Minister Chris not only pours out her love for her children, but also a host of others whom God has entrusted to her. Her life verses are: "May Christ through your faith [actually] dwell (settle down, abide, make His permanent home) in your hearts! May you be rooted deep in love and founded securely on love, That you may have the power and be strong to apprehend and grasp with all the saints [God's devoted people, the experience of that love] what is the breadth and length and height and depth [of it]; [That you may really come] to know [practically, through experience for yourselves] the love of Christ, which far surpasses mere knowledge [without experience]; that you may be filled [through all your being] unto all the fullness of God [may have the richest measure of the divine Presence, and become a body wholly filled and flooded with God Himself]!" Eph. 3:17-19 (AMPC)

Minister Chris is a member of Sharon Bible Fellowship Church in Lanham, Maryland, under the leadership of Pastor Victor O. Kirk, Sr. and the mentorship of Pastor Berry Watkins. She has poured her heart into ministry roles (current and former) such as Leader of I'm Full "The Singles" Ministry, Praise & Worship Team, Life Group Facilitator, Choir Member, Christian Education Teacher, Bible Institute Instructor, Women's Ministry, and Leader of Social Media Ministry.

Contact

Website: restorationspeaks.com
Twitter & Instagram: awic4chris
Facebook: Chris Allen
Facebook: Restoration Speaks
Twitter & Instagram: @Chris4Bling

WON'T HE DO IT?

I just want to inform you all that I am the one who created the saying, "Won't He Do It?" For real though, I am going to claim that whether I am or not. LOL! So, just go along with it, okay?

God has been so good to me and my family that it is so hard to know where to start. I could start with healings of our family, or financial blessings, or tell about when he showed up right on time in ministry. Time and time again he has shown up and showed out.

I can remember back in the day when my youngest daughter was born, and I was working in the accounting department at the church I was attending. I had my daughter and felt led to stay home and take care of her because I could not find suitable Christian childcare. I prayed about staying home because in the natural we could not afford for me to do this. Now that we were a family of five it did not seem feasible. Well, we went to vote at the voting polls and had our baby with us in the carrier and while standing in the line; a lady in

WON'T HE DO IT

front of us looked at the baby and said, "Oh I have lots of baby stuff that you can have if you would like to come to my house and pick it up. Well, of course we said that we would come to pick it up. She gave us her address, which was about a block away from our house, Bless God! We went to pick up the items. She had everything that we could have needed for our baby. There was formula, bottles, baby blankets, clothes, diapers, etc. Every need was met!! Won't He Do It!? Yes, He will!!

Then the Lord blessed me with how to make income and take care of our baby at the same time. I started to do childcare from my home. Every source of income that is legal is a good source of income as long as you are willing to do it to the best of your ability. My kids and I love children, so a family daycare was a great idea and blessing. Well, one day a horrendous thing happened. I was babysitting a three-month-old baby girl. I put her down for her nap and after an allotted time went to wake her for changing and feeding. I picked up a lifeless baby in my arms. 911 was called while I administered CPR. The rescue team did get the baby breathing again. The mother drove up just as they were driving away with her baby and they let her in to ride along with them. The baby did die later on after arriving at the hospital. This was a trying time because you know that there is always a feeling of what did I do wrong? Is this my fault? What happened here? There was an investigation of me and the parents. It was found that the baby passed away from crib death. Praise be to God that he kept the parents and my family and I too. He wiped away all of the guilt and fear. The parents were able to hug and love on me as I was to do the same to them! God had showed up and showed out again!! Won't He Do It?

God is an Awesome God!! He may not come when you want Him but, He is always on time. We went through a very serious financial slump, and we were on the very verge of losing our home. We were standing on the word of God alone. We had decided that if we lose our home we will stand and trust God that he had better for us. God was and is always in control and we have to learn to trust him at all times. Hebrews 11:6 tells us that without faith it is impossible to please him. We were down to the final weekend before being put out on Monday. I remember very distinctively saying to my friends/co-workers that we were moving over the weekend. So, they were asking why and where etc. So, I shared with them what was happening. Well, low and behold after hearing what was going on with us losing our home and how they had seen me come to work like nothing was going on day after day because of standing on the Word of God, they voluntarily asked how much I needed, called their husbands and asked how much they could give. And they gave me the money that day to save our home from foreclosure!! Look at God!! I said they voluntarily offered the money. I did not ask them. You know that was nobody but God!! He will make a way out of no way!! Won't He Do It?

That's one of the reasons I love the song, "Waymaker." That is exactly who He is to us!! Just as He is the "Great I Am", "Emmanuel", "Lily of the Valley", "Wheel in the middle of a wheel", "Alpha and Omega", "The beginning and the end".

WON'T HE DO IT

He's a lawyer in the courtroom, a doctor in the sick room, waymaker, miracle worker, promise keeper; my God that is who you are!! Thank You Jesus!! Won't He Do It?

Time and time again God has shown up and created a Blessing out of what the devil meant for a cursing. God has shown the devil to be a liar at all times. There is no greater Love than the Love that God has for us. He has given us everything that we need to succeed.

We moved from N.C. to Maryland in 1987. LaKesha was 5 years old and decided one day to take a walk by herself. In the country of N.C. where we moved from it was nothing to walk from our house to grandma's house, but even then, she wasn't old enough to walk alone. So, she decided she would walk to a friend's house that we had met in Maryland. So, she walked out of our complex and onto a main road toward the friend's house. I thought she had walked to where her dad was around the corner working on a car. When he came home without her we looked all over the complex and checked with kids she might have played with and could not find her anywhere. We called the police. This was one of the scariest times in our lives as parents. We had no idea what to think and the list of things that could happen to our baby was too long to even try to be calm. Hours went by and finally the police found her not too far from our house. A man had seen her walking alone and had taken her hand and asked her to lead him to her home. So, they were headed back to our house. Thank God for that man because it could have been another type of man. He was helping and not hurting our daughter!! Look at God!! Our child was returned to us safe and sound with no hurt, harm, or danger!! Won't He Do It?

I'm so glad that God loves us unconditionally. He loves us right on through our mess and even when we fail to do what He would have us to do at times. God cares for us even more than we care for ourselves. He knows the amount of hairs on our head according to Luke 12:7! We need to be in continual prayer and praise with Him at all times.

God bought our family through a nightmare of many years of sheer Hell. I married an alcoholic at the age of 16 and he was 29. Never knew he was an alcoholic even when all the signs were there. My little 16-year-old mind told me that he was the one for me, and when I married, I married for life. So, even in the midst of verbal, mental, and physical abuse, I was determined to stay married. This was going on even before I had given my life to Christ. My husband would miss weeks of work at a time, and we wouldn't know if he was alive or dead. He threw away entire paychecks like it was nothing. I had to work hard to keep our heads above water and keep food on the table for my children. We were so ashamed of anyone coming to our house to visit because we never knew when he would be sober or drunk. He would call me every name in the book from Hell! You know these were not good nor Godly names! I would end up hurt sometimes from his attempt to make me fear him. Often in his stupor he would end up making a mistake of actually hitting me or breaking something that would shatter and cut me like a liquor bottle or something. A lot of times I feared going to work at night

WON'T HE DO IT

and leaving my kids with him. I got a call at work many times about Kesha getting burned on a wood stove; falling on a nail and getting a gash in her head and having to leave work to go to the hospital. When I say the nightmare from Hell, it was literally that. My kids had no other choice but to become mature and keepers of themselves when I had to work. I Praise God that He didn't allow them to grow up to hate me for keeping them in that madness. I can't even tell you the amount of years it lasted. God had a plan. One day after being tired of being tired; I turned on my husband! After that day there was never another day that he put his hands on me accidently or otherwise. One part of the madness was over. Then when I decided to give my life fully to Christ, I thought that it would be better soon but, it was not. I felt that if I had put up with so many years of it without Christ that knowing Christ would make it end soon. Well, God wanted me to grow and learn how to trust Him no matter what; and that's what happened. I felt like I was done and there was no help for the marriage and I was looking for a place to move with my older children by now. But, because of God's plan I could not find anywhere to go. So, once I just gave it all to God; He took over. I had finally let go and let God. I had to take my hands off of the situation entirely. I stopped pouring out his liquor, stopped looking for him when he was missing, stopped fussing with him, stopped listening to his verbal abuse. I stopped being a victim. I started to pray and trust God to guide my steps. To trust God to do what only He could do. My way had failed miserably, and we were spiraling downward at an amazing speed. My husband had been in substance abuse programs time and time again and he would complete the program only to go right back to drinking. Finally, after I had let God have it, I started noticing day after day was going by and my husband wasn't getting drunk. I was so amazed. We could not believe it and did not want to get our hopes up, so we didn't dare mention it to him that we noticed. God was doing what He said He would do and answering prayer and it was a shock right before our eyes. Time went by and before we knew it; it had been more than a year of sobriety for my husband. We had a celebration at our house with our church family to let him know that we were happy, and that God had done a great thing in our lives. I am happy to let you know that it has been over 12 years since God completed that work in my husband. Glory Hallelujah!! Won't He Do It? Yes, He Will!!

My husband had also been a smoker from a very young age. But, three years after God took the alcohol spirit from him, God took the cigarette smoking from him immediately. There were no withdrawal periods, no slowly letting it get out of his system. God said that's enough, my husband wanted Him to take those spirits and God did just that! Immediately!! Wont He Do It? This is the kind of God we serve!! He is no respecter of persons. He will do the same for anybody else that he did for my husband. He is Omnipotent!! He speaks and everything and everybody listens, because what He speaks will come forth!! The same way He spoke to the waves when Peter walked out of the boat onto the water; He spoke to them and said, "Peace be still." He is the same God today that He was yesterday, tomorrow, and forever more!! Try Him for yourself!! He is waiting with open arms!! Thank you, Jesus!!!

WON'T HE DO IT

So, yes, I know the true meaning of "Won't He Do It?" That's why I claim the rights to it!! I could go on and on about the healings of several different cancers that attacked my husband, and how today He is cancer-free in the name of Jesus. They call cancer the big "C", but my God is the big "G". I could tell you about all the things that God has headed, and still is healing in my body but, I don't have the time to tell it all in this one sitting!! But, know that I know a man that is a Way Maker, Miracle Worker, Promise Keeper!! To God be all the Honor, Glory, and Praise!! Won't He Do It? Yes, He Will!!

About Doris M. Williams

Doris M. Williams is known as a loving mother, faithful Nana, supportive wife and a loyal friend. Many have the pleasure to know her as a worshipper and a diligent prayer warrior. Often called Mama Doris, her motherly and loving demeanor is one of the first things that people encounter upon meeting her. Born and raised in Dunn, North Carolina, Doris is the mother of two beautiful daughters and one son with her loving husband, Cleo Williams. Cleo and Doris just recently celebrated 40 years of marriage, which is something she truly prides herself on. After retiring from her twenty-year career in Accounting and working with the DC government, Doris also attained her B.S. in Business Administration and a master's degree in Human Services: Marriage and Family Counseling. She is a true believer, a supporter of all whom she loves, and a woman purely after God's heart. This shines through in her every day walk of life.

Contact

Email: dorprayer@aol.com
FB: https://www.facebook.com/doris.williams.58
IG: @GodsDivaD

Doris' Acknowledgements

I would like to acknowledge the founder of Vision to Fruition!! Not just because she is my daughter, but because God has gifted her with great and awesome tools for His kingdom and she wears the tool belt well. She is a loyal, dedicated, hard worker that aims for the very best at all times for all the people she works with and most definitely her family!! I am so very proud of all of her accomplishments and so very happy that God chose me to be her mom!! She is the epitome of "BLACK GIRL MAGIC!" LAKESHA ROCKS!!!

OUR HOPE

For His Spirit joins with our spirit to affirm that we are God's children. And since we are His children, we are His heirs. In fact, together with Christ, we are heirs of God's glory. But if we are to share His glory, we must also share His suffering. Yet what we suffer now is nothing compared to the glory He will reveal to us later.
Romans 8:16-18

John 16:33 says, "*These things I have spoken to you, so that in Me you may have peace. In the world you have tribulation but take courage; I have overcome the world.*" With these words, Jesus told His disciples to take courage because, despite the inevitable struggles they would face, they would not be alone, as you have seen through the testimonies you have just read. Jesus does not abandon us to our struggles either. If we remember that the ultimate victory has already been won, we can claim the peace of following Christ can be challenging in the most troublesome times. Jesus was unmistakably confident that the choice to follow Him would not be easy or free from struggle.

First John 5:4-5 says, "For whatever is born of God overcomes the world; and this is the victory that has overcome the world—our faith. Who is the one who overcomes the world, but he who believes that Jesus is the Son of God?"

Are you living like an Overcomer? The very process of overcoming implies that there is a struggle. The beauty of the struggle is becoming an overcomer. God wants to use the struggle to push you towards Him.

The key is to take on the spirit of an overcomer and "come over" those mountains that you face. Galatians 6:9 reveals the profile of an overcomer, "Let us not lose heart in doing good, for in due time we will reap if we do not grow weary." It is discouraging to continue to do right and receive no word of thanks or see no tangible results. But Paul challenged the Galatians as he challenges us to keep on doing good and to trust God for the results. In due time, we will reap a harvest of blessing.

An Overcomer:
1. Refuses to grow weary.
2. Keeps on doing good.
3. Recognizes their due season is coming.
4. Is committed to reaping.
5. Does not lose heart.

What specific challenge are you facing today? If you look at this situation through these characteristics of an overcomer, how would it change the way you see things?

An overcomer's perspective is from the top of the "mountain" instead of the bottom. When you understand that the Greater One lives in you and gives you the power to overcome, you change your standpoint. Below you will find the eight rewards of overcoming found in Revelation.

1. Revelation 2:7 – "He who has an ear, let Him hear what the Spirit says to the churches. To him who overcomes, I will grant to eat of the tree of life which is in the Paradise of God." To overcome is to be victorious by believing in Christ, persevering, remaining faithful and living as one who follows Christ. Such a life brings hope and great rewards.

2. Revelation 2:11 - "He who has an ear, let him hear what the Spirit says to the churches. He who overcomes will not be hurt by the second death." Pain is a part of life, but it is never easy to suffer, no matter what the cause. Jesus commended the church at Smyrna for its faith in suffering. He then encouraged the believers that they need not fear the future if they remained faithful. If you are experiencing difficult times, don't let them turn you away from God. Instead, let them draw you toward greater faithfulness. Trust God and remember your heavenly reward.

3. Revelation 2:17 - "He who has an ear, let him hear what the Spirit says to the churches. To him who overcomes, to him, I will give some of the hidden manna, and I will give him a white

stone, and a new name written on the stone which no one knows but he who receives it." The "Hidden manna" suggests the spiritual nourishment that the faithful believers will receive. As the Israelites traveled toward the promised land, God provided manna from heaven for their physical nourishment. Jesus, as the bread of life, provides spiritual nourishment that satisfies our deepest hunger. It is unclear what the white stones are or exactly what the names on each will be but because they relate to the hidden manna, they may be symbols of the believer's eternal nourishment or eternal life. The stones are significant because each will bear the new name of every person who truly believes in Christ. They are the evidence that a person has overcome and been accepted by God and declared worthy to receive eternal life. A person's name represented his or her character. God will give us new names and new hearts.

4. Revelation 2:25-28 – "Nevertheless what you have, hold fast until I come. He who overcomes, and he who keeps My deeds until the end, to him I will give authority over the nations; and he shall rule them with a rod of iron, as the vessels of the potter are broken to pieces, as I also have received authority from My Father; and I will give him the morning star." We should hold tightly to the basics of our Christian faith and view with caution and counsel any new teaching that turns us away from the Bible, the fellowship of our church, or our basic confession of faith. Christ says that those who overcome (those who remain faithful until the end and continue to please God) will rule over Christ's enemies and reign with Him as He judges evil.

5. Revelation 3:5 – "He who overcomes will thus be clothed in white garments, and I will not erase his name from the book of life, and I will confess his name before My Father and before His angels." To be "clothed in white garments" means to be set apart for God and made pure. Christ promises future honor and eternal life to those who stand firm in their faith. The names of all believers are registered in the book of life. This book symbolizes God's knowledge of who belongs to Him. All such people are guaranteed a listing in the book of life and are introduced to the hosts of heaven as belonging to Christ.

6. Revelation 3:12 - "He who overcomes, I will make him a pillar in the temple of My God, and he will not go out from it anymore; and I will write on him the name of My God, and the name of the city of My God, the new Jerusalem, which comes down out of heaven from My God, and My new name." The new Jerusalem is the future dwelling of the people of God. We will have a new citizenship in God's future kingdom. Everything will be new, pure and secure.

7. Revelation 3:21 – "He who overcomes, I will grant to him to sit down with Me on My throne, as I also overcame and sat down with My Father on His throne." God is faithful to His children, and although we may suffer great hardships here, God promises that someday we will live eternally with Him.

8. Revelation 21:7-8 – "He who overcomes will inherit these things, and I will be his God and he will be My son. But for the cowardly and unbelieving and abominable and murderers and immoral persons and sorcerers and idolaters and all liars,

their part will be in the lake that burns with fire and brimstone, which is the second death." The "cowardly" are not those who are fainthearted in their faith or who sometimes doubt or question, but those who turn back from following God. They are not brave enough to stand up for Christ; they are not humble enough to accept His authority over their lives. They are put on the same list as the unbelieving, the vile, the murderers, the liars, the idolaters, the sexually immoral and the practicing of magic arts.

People who overcome endure "to the end." They will receive the rewards that God promised: (1) eating from the tree of life, (2) escaping the lake of fire, (3) receiving a special name, (4) having authority over the nations, (5) being included in the book of life, (6) being a pillar in God's spiritual temple, (7) sitting with Christ on His throne and (8) a heavenly inheritance. Those who can endure the testing of evil, remain faithful and overcome will be rewarded by God.

So again, I ask, are you living like an Overcomer? Do you feel like an Overcomer? "Come on over" whatever you're facing today, start living life victoriously in Christ and wait with great anticipation to reap the rewards of overcoming, that is our hope!

CONCLUSION

"I have told you all this so that you may have peace in me. Here on earth, you will have many trials and sorrows. But take heart, because I have overcome the world."
John 16:33

It is my desire that because of reading this book, an awareness has been awakened and a boldness has been activated within you. The stories we've shared in this book have been snippets of things we have gone through in life. We shared our testimonies in hopes that they would be the catalyst to initiate a chain reaction of hope. What I mean is anything that happens to you or that you are currently going through in your life should elicit a response of peace because you know God has equipped you with what I call the Overcomers Gene.

The Overcomers Gene is a part of our Divine DNA, when we were adopted into the body of Christ, this gene came alive. Before our adoption into the Body of Christ this gene was recessive but when we confess our sins, accept Jesus Christ as our Lord and Savior, begin following Him, and God filled us with the Holy Spirit; the indwelling of the Holy Spirit activated this gene.

The goal of this book and Born Overcomers, Inc., is to win souls for Christ and to simply help people believe they were Born to Overcome! Do you believe?

God loves you unconditionally, His desire is that you would find your identity in Him, love Him, trust Him and tell others about Him. No matter your past or your current situation, God holds your future and you were born to overcome!

BELIEVE IT!
LIVE IT!
WALK IN IT!
TELL SOMEONE ELSE ABOUT IT!

About the Publisher

At Vision to Fruition, we are dedicated to helping others bring their personal, business, ministry & nonprofit visions to fruition.

Whether it's as grand as a book you want to write, a business you want to start, a conference or event you want to host, a ministry you want to launch or an organization you want to start; or as small as needing a computer repair, logo design or web design; Vision to Fruition will help you walk through the process and set you up for success! At Vision to Fruition we don't have clients, we have Visionaries. We provide solutions to equip others to pursue their visions & dreams with reckless abandon.

LaKesha is the Lead Visionary behind Overcomers HQ, which is dedicated to helping others overcome, thrive & bring their visions to fruition. OHQ is comprised of Born Overcomers Inc., Vision to Fruition, LaKesha L. Williams Ministries, Team Overcomers & Overcomers Bling.

In 2018 we have published seven authors, two of which were Amazon Best Sellers. We would love for you to join our family of Visionaries as well!!!

Learn more here www.vision-fruition.com

www.ingramcontent.com/pod-product-compliance
Lightning Source LLC
Chambersburg PA
CBHW051057160426
43193CB00010B/1220